T0331193

Empirical Social Choice

Since Aristotle, many different theories of distributive justice have been proposed, by philosophers as well as by social scientists. The typical approach within social choice theory is to assess these theories in an axiomatic way – most of the time the reader is confronted with abstract reasoning and logical deductions. This book shows that empirical insights are necessary if one wants to apply any theory of justice in the real world. It does so by confronting the main theories of distributive justice with data from (mostly) questionnaire experiments. The book starts with an extensive discussion on why empirical social choice makes sense, and how it should be done. It then presents various experimental results relating to theories of distributive justice, including the Rawlsian equity axiom, Harsanyi's version of utilitarianism, utilitarianism with a floor, responsibility-sensitive egalitarianism, the claims problem and fairness in health.

WULF GAERTNER is Professor of Economics at the University of Osnabrück. He is also a visiting professor at the London School of Economics. He is the author of *Domain Conditions in Social Choice Theory* (Cambridge University Press, 2001) and *A Primer in Social Choice Theory* (Revised edition, 2009).

ERIK SCHOKKAERT is Full Professor in Public Economics at Katholieke Universiteit Leuven and Research Director at CORE, Université catholique de Louvain.

Empirical Social Choice

Questionnaire–Experimental Studies on Distributive Justice

WULF GAERTNER

AND

ERIK SCHOKKAERT

CAMBRIDGE
UNIVERSITY PRESS

CAMBRIDGE
UNIVERSITY PRESS

University Printing House, Cambridge CB2 8BS, United Kingdom

One Liberty Plaza, 20th Floor, New York, NY 10006, USA

477 Williamstown Road, Port Melbourne, VIC 3207, Australia

314-321, 3rd Floor, Plot 3, Splendor Forum, Jasola District Centre, New Delhi - 110025, India

79 Anson Road, #06-04/06, Singapore 079906

Cambridge University Press is part of the University of Cambridge.

It furthers the University's mission by disseminating knowledge in the pursuit of
education, learning and research at the highest international levels of excellence.

www.cambridge.org
Information on this title: www.cambridge.org/9781107013940

First published 2012

A catalogue record for this publication is available from the British Library

Library of Congress Cataloging in Publication data
Gaertner, Wulf.
Empirical social choice : questionnaire–experimental studies on distributive
justice / Wulf Gaertner, Erik Schokkaert.
    p. cm.
Includes index.
ISBN 978-1-107-01394-0
1. Social choice. 2. Distributive justice. I. Schokkaert, Erik. II. Title.
HB846.8.G343   2012
302'.13–dc23
2011026096

ISBN 978-1-107-01394-0 Hardback

Contents

Figures

Tables

Acknowledgements

We are very grateful to Kristof Bosmans, who kindly read the complete manuscript and made various valuable suggestions. We also wish to thank all our former PhD students and colleagues who, over many years, did joint work with us on empirical social choice. This collaboration has been most stimulating and productive for us. Finally, our thanks go to Chris Harrison and his staff of Cambridge University Press for their help and support.

We dedicate this book to our families.

I   Introduction

In his *Nicomachean Ethics*, Aristotle wrote that 'both the unjust man and the unjust act are unfair or unequal, and clearly in each case of inequality there is something intermediate, viz., that which is equal... Then if what is unjust is unequal, what is just is equal.' Justice is here defined as equality. However, Aristotle continued, saying that 'a just act necessarily involves at least four terms: two persons for whom it is in fact just, and two shares in which its justice is exhibited. And there will be the same equality between the shares as between the persons, because the shares will be in the same ratio to one another as the persons; for if the persons are not equal, they will not have equal shares; and it is when equals have or are assigned unequal shares, or people who are not equal, equal shares, that quarrels and complaints break out' (fourth century BC, 1976, pp. 177–8). Therefore, Aristotle viewed 'equality' as a kind of proportion. 'What is just ... is what is proportional, and what is unjust is what violates the proportion. So one share becomes too large and the other too small. This is exactly what happens in practice: the man who acts unjustly gets too much and the victim of injustice too little of what is good' (1976, p. 179).

Since Aristotle, many different theories of distributive justice have been proposed, by philosophers as well as by social scientists. Moreover, the content of justice is an essential ingredient of the political debate in many countries. Ideas of proportionality and equality have kept playing an important role in these discussions. However, both ideas remain empty as long as one does not define explicitly what the variables are that have to be in proportion or what it is that has to be distributed equally. The real debate is then about the following questions that we consider as basic. Should a just income distribution correct for differences in needs and, if yes, how? Should one take into account differences in tastes, or in the capacity to enjoy various goods, as proposed by utilitarianism? Should differences in productivity be rewarded? Should we distinguish between productivity differences reflecting differences in natural talent and those reflecting effort? More generally, how should aspects of responsibility and desert be integrated? And what about historical or legal claims?

There are two strands in the academic and scientific literature on these topics. One approach, most popular among psychologists and sociologists, is descriptive. It looks at prevailing opinions in society and tries to explain where they come from and how they are distributed over various social groups. From this perspective, justice is a social construct that is impossible to universalize and is unavoidably culture- and time-dependent. The other approach, most popular among philosophers, is normative. It tries to reason about the nature of justice by putting forward and evaluating different rational arguments. There is hardly any contact between these two strands of literature. The former claims that 'the perennial search for the true meaning of justice has not been particularly fruitful, and it is likely that there is no true or essential justice beyond its socially constructed meanings' (Törnblom, 1992, p. 178). The latter emphasizes that 'empirical ethics is inconsistent with the very nature of moral judgments, which are supposed to be rationally contestable, because it implies that the social consensus is always right, and minority views and the views of social reformers are always automatically mistaken ... Such a view clashes with the actual practice of moral argument and seems to leave no room for rational contestation of moral disagreements' (Hausman, 2000, p. 40).

Welfare economics and social choice theory have to be placed among the normative approaches to distributive justice. In some sense they can be seen as a form of applied ethics, using the same basic approach as moral and political philosophy. There may be some difference in emphasis, as economists traditionally are more concerned about the trade-off between efficiency and justice, and therefore about the distinction between 'optimal' and 'just' allocations. Moreover, the economic approach is in general more formalized and it uses a mathematical style of argument. In recent decades, the axiomatic approach has become especially popular (Thomson, 2001). Yet, there can be no doubt that the ultimate goal of the theory is normative.

It is therefore remarkable that in recent decades there has been an increase of papers in what could be called 'empirical social choice'. The seminal paper by Yaari and Bar-Hillel (1984) is the archetypical example of the whole approach. The two authors studied the concept of justice or just distribution via 'judgments of justice', elicited from hypothetical questions. More specifically, the authors gave students hypothetical distribution problems and asked them 'to solve them justly' (Bar-Hillel and Yaari, 1993, p. 59). Their aim is not descriptive as they emphasize that the focus of their research is the ethical notions in people's minds, not their actual behaviour, keeping in mind that actual behaviour 'is inevitably contaminated by political, strategic, and other considerations' (1993, p. 59). They add that 'it is people's expressed sentiments (namely what they say ought to be done) rather than their revealed ones (namely what they actually do) that primarily guides the search for a *normative* theory of justice, as well as the rhetoric of public debate on issues of distributive justice' (1993, p. 59). Contrary to the work in psychology and sociology, Yaari and Bar-Hillel deliberately use the insights from normative economic theory to structure the questions that are proposed to the respondents. Contrary to the opinion of most philosophers, they suggest that such empirical work may make a useful contribution to building a normative theory.

Given the sharp distinction that has traditionally been made between empirical and normative approaches, it is not surprising that the methodological arguments of Yaari and Bar-Hillel are far from being generally accepted. We will go more deeply into these basic questions in Chapter 2, in which we will also describe the main methodological features of the work on empirical social choice. The bulk of the book then consists of a discussion of typical studies. We will first summarize in Chapter 3 some results which are mainly relevant to questions in the Arrovian social choice tradition: the acceptability of welfarism, of the Pareto principle and of the concept of the veil of ignorance. We will then turn in Chapter 4 to issues that have come up in the recent approach of fair allocation in economic environments: the possibilities and limitations of responsibility-sensitive egalitarianism and the relevance of different solutions to the claims problem. Chapter 5 focuses on one specific but rich field of application: that of fairness in health and health care delivery. Chapter 6 concludes.

It is not our aim to give a complete overview of the empirical work on distributive justice. As explained in Chapter 2, we omit the bulk of the rapidly growing literature on game-theory-based laboratory experiments. Moreover, we restrict ourselves to papers that are relevant to social choice, as it is usually defined. We do not discuss the large amount of work on the acceptance of different approaches to the measurement of inequality (Amiel and Cowell, 1999) or on the acceptance of market arrangements (see, e.g., the seminal paper by Kahneman et al., 1986). Even within the social choice literature, we do not aim at completeness. We do not discuss experiments on voting behaviour. Moreover, we prefer to describe a restricted set of representative studies in detail, to illustrate the pros and cons of the methodology and to show its relevance for social choice. A more comprehensive survey, that also incorporates findings from sociological and psychological studies, can be found in Konow (2003).

2 Empirical social choice: why and how?

As described in Chapter 1, there are two strands in the literature on distributive justice: one descriptive, the other normative. The existence of these two strands as such does not raise a real intellectual challenge. Indeed, one could keep to the traditional Humean distinction and simply accept that they tackle two basically different but potentially interesting questions. The first question is positive: what are the feelings and attitudes in society with respect to distributive justice, and how are these linked to the individual and social characteristics of the respondents? The other one is ethical: which arguments are valid for defining a 'just' situation or a 'just' society? In this dichotomic view, the two approaches can (and should) remain completely separate. Ethical theories are usually much more subtle and complex than everyday opinions and the former can therefore be very misleading as a guide to the latter. There is a real danger that a survey based on these ethical theories would be far removed from any relevant psychological reality of lay citizens. On the other hand, a specific perspective on distributive justice does not become ethically acceptable just because it is supported by a majority of the population. Therefore, in this dichotomic view, positive and normative approaches can easily co-exist. A real challenge only arises if one goes beyond the dichotomy and argues that the descriptive and the normative approach cannot only co-exist, but are complementary and mutually enriching. One then has to show either that ethical theories can be helpful for the empirical work, or that the empirical results can be useful for ethical reasoning, or both.

The challenge is real for 'empirical social choice'. Social choice makes use of an axiomatic approach to define ethically attractive solutions to situations in which there is a distributional conflict or a trade-off between equity and efficiency. The approach is aptly summarized by Luce and Raiffa (1957, p. 121), as follows:

> Rather than dream up a multitude of arbitration schemes and determine whether or not each withstands the best of plausibility in a host of special cases, let us invert the procedure. Let us examine our subjective intuition of fairness and formulate this as a set of precise desiderata that any acceptable arbitration scheme must fulfil. Once these desiderata are formalized as axioms, then the problem is reduced to a mathematical investigation of the existence of and characterization of arbitration schemes which satisfy the axioms.

The last part of the quote seems to suggest that social choice is no more than a purely formal exercise. Indeed, some theorists have taken the position that its main purpose is simply to explore the logical relationships between the various axioms, rather than discussing their normative implications (Maniquet, 1999). However, in a broader interpretation (which, we feel, is supported by the largest part of the profession), the purpose of axiomatic social choice is precisely normative, i.e. to determine which schemes are unfair and which are ethically acceptable. Luce and Raiffa (1957, p. 123) continue:

> By means of a (small) finite number of axioms, we are able to 'examine' the infinity of possible schemes, *to throw away those which are unfair, and to characterize those which are acceptable.* The only alternative – to examine in detail each of the infinity of schemes for each of the infinity of possible conflicts it is supposed to arbitrate – is not practical [our italics].

The power of the axiomatic approach resides precisely in the possibility of separating two questions. Exploring the first question about the logical relationships between the various axioms is a branch of applied mathematics. Yet applied mathematics cannot answer the second, ethical, question about the fairness of different solutions. The separation allows us to rephrase the 'why' question of this chapter. It is obvious that empirical work is completely useless for solving the logical problems. The interesting question is whether it can yield useful insights into the ethical acceptability of specific axioms or specific solutions. In fact, the axiomatic approach offers a possible way out of the dilemma that philosophically attractive theories are too complicated to be submitted to the population. Focusing on the separate axioms or specific solutions themselves allows the empirical researcher to formulate questions which are theoretically meaningful and at the same time understandable for the population at large. Axiomatic social choice theory reduces the intricate reasoning of a complete ethical theory to its essential constitutive building blocks. The two questions posed in this chapter can now be reformulated. Is it meaningful to investigate the social acceptance of specific axioms and specific solution concepts? How should one collect the relevant empirical information to investigate this social acceptance?

Note that we only discuss the question whether empirical work can be relevant for the formulation of normative theories and leave aside the opposite relationship, i.e. whether the insights from social choice can be useful to structure the descriptive work on opinions about distributive justice. We think they can, as they may help to overcome the 'feeling of intellectual disorganization' (Deutsch, 1983), which characterizes some of the empirical work (see also Bell and Schokkaert, 1992). However, this argument is beyond the scope of the present book.

2.1   WHY EMPIRICAL SOCIAL CHOICE?

Some have taken the position that there can be no good normative theory of justice without strong empirical foundations. However, there is no need to go that far if one wants to defend the usefulness of empirical social choice. In this section, we will first introduce some easily acceptable arguments and then move gradually to the more debatable ones. First, empirical insights are necessary if one wants to apply any theory of justice in the real world. Second, they may point to biases in the existing approaches and, third, they may suggest interesting questions and puzzles. Fourth, in some cases they may be complementary to theory, in the sense that they are needed to fill in gaps. Finally, we will come back to the position that a normative debate is only meaningful if it incorporates the empirical results about opinions prevailing in society.

2.1.1 Towards application of social choice

One good reason to do science is mere intellectual curiosity. However, in the case of normative theory this can hardly be sufficient. The ultimate aim of any normative theory must be to be put into practice. Thinking about the content of justice without the desire of making the world more just, is like pouring out a glass of water and then refusing to drink.[1] Yet, in a political democracy it is nearly impossible to implement any theory of justice without sufficient support from the general public. This support will depend on the citizens' own values and preferences. Empirical research on the acceptance of notions of justice by different social groups is therefore essential to understand the social environment in which policy decisions are taken. As an example, suppose (realistically, as will be shown in subsequent chapters) that for a majority of citizens subjective utilities are not the exclusive nor even the most important criterion for evaluating policies. In that case, a utilitarian economist will have a hard time putting some of his specific policy proposals into practice. Certainly, even if this utilitarian economist does not start doubting his utilitarian convictions, he would benefit from a better understanding of the structure of opinions in society.

That social values play a role in shaping economic policy is now well understood. Figure 2.1 (taken from Alesina and Angeletos, 2005) offers an interesting illustration. The figure shows a significant positive relationship at the cross-country level between the percentage of respondents who believe that income is mainly determined by luck rather than by effort (on the horizontal axis) and social spending as a % of GDP (on the vertical axis). Of course, the positive relationship in the figure is only a suggestion that attitudes influence policies. Causality

---

[1] We paraphrase Samuelson (1947, p. 249) who used the same formulation in the context of making interpersonal comparisons.

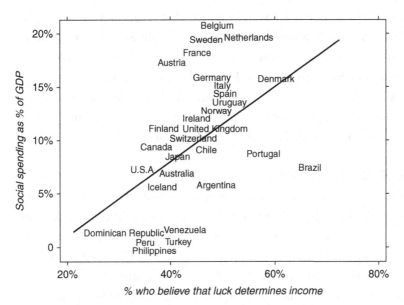

FIGURE 2.1 Social values and social spending (Alesina and Angeletos, 2005)

also runs in the opposite direction, with the percentage of social spending influencing both the justice perceptions of individuals and the link between luck and income in the real world.[2] Yet, the example is sufficient to suggest that empirical work on opinions may help to understand reality – and to shape economic policy. Note, moreover, that the Alesina–Angeletos model explicitly assumes that the distinction between luck and effort is meaningful for the formulation of a theory of justice. This is the (non-welfarist) starting point of some recent theories of fair allocation, to which we will return in Chapter 4.

In this line of thinking, empirical work is meaningful, even if one rejects emphatically the idea that the popularity of a specific notion of justice in the population has some relevance for its ethical respectability. Even if one considers the majority opinions to be ethically

---

[2] This idea of reciprocal influence is the key idea behind the equilibrium concept in the theoretical model of Alesina and Angeletos (2005).

unacceptable, one still has to convince a sufficient number of citizens if one wants to implement one's own supposedly superior conception of justice. To build a convincing case, a better insight into the structure of the uninformed opinions, that have 'to be corrected', may be extremely useful, even necessary. All this also implies that a minimal requirement for a theory of justice must be that it can be explained to the members of society. If not, public support for it is highly doubtful.

2.1.2 Correcting biases

Empirical research consistently shows that individual justice opinions are linked to personal characteristics. Let us again give an example which does not come from the social choice tradition. Alesina and Giuliano (2011) analyse the preferences for redistribution in the US on the basis of the General Social Survey. They find that (after controlling for family income and age), more educated individuals are more averse to redistribution and that the opposite holds for women, for blacks and for respondents with a history of misfortune (e.g. unemployment) or those that have been raised Catholic or Jewish. Moreover, the willingness to redistribute interacts with ideas about and perceptions of fairness, such as the relative importance of hard work versus luck or the degree of equality of opportunity (see also Fong, 2001). Confront these findings with the profile of a modal social choice theorist. This modal social choice theorist is male, with a university degree, with an income well above average but at the same time well below the top, individualistic and intellectually ambitious. The probability that he is black is much smaller than it is for the overall population, the probability that he is Jewish is much larger. Unless social choice theorists in one way or another escape from the psychological regularities which characterize the attitudes of all other citizens, it seems likely that their atypical profile will be reflected in the theories they propose. Of course, social choice theorists are well aware that impartiality is an essential component of justice, but a greater awareness of social influences (also on their own frame of thinking) could certainly help to make them more careful about this.

The specific methodology of social choice raises some additional issues. Social choice theorists are part of a scientific community where model-building skills are highly rewarded and where the ability to formulate a problem in mathematical terms helps very much in being taken seriously. This is a good thing, as the formalized axiomatic approach undoubtedly yields insights which could not be obtained by any other method. Yet, at the same time, there is the danger that the availability of techniques partly determines the research agenda. Empirical research may then confront theorists with the possible trade-off between technical sophistication and social relevance.

There is another aspect of the methodology which should be mentioned. When discussing the acceptability of axioms or the applicability of specific models, theorists often refer to typical cases. They like to tell simple stories about shipwrecked people in a lifeboat or about sons dividing the bequest of their father. There is nothing wrong with focusing on specific stories in order to sharpen one's intuitions. However, the ultimate purpose of the approach is to derive conclusions with a broader scope. Again, there is a danger here. As we will see in later chapters of this book, empirical research shows that ethical intuitions are context-dependent. It seems to matter whether one thinks about sons dividing a bequest, or about anonymous creditors of a bankrupt firm. The ethical requirements imposed on old friends in a lifeboat may be different from those imposed on complete strangers. Irrespective of whether this context-dependence is a real component of justice or a mere framing effect to be corrected for, the theorist should better be aware of it in order to avoid drawing general conclusions on the basis of overly narrow examples.

2.1.3 Suggesting interesting puzzles

The message of the last examples from subsection 2.1.2 can also be formulated in a more constructive way. Rather than merely pointing to biases which are to be avoided, empirical results may in addition act as an eye-opener and suggest new and interesting avenues for theoretical reasoning. Findings with respect to context-dependence may be especially relevant in this regard. Suppose one formulates two specific stories which are identical in all aspects that are relevant within a given theory. The stories differ, however, in some respects which should not matter according to theory. Suppose now that the justice perceptions of the respondents are different in these two stories. There are then two possible interpretations. One is that the response differences reflect irrelevant framing effects and should not be taken seriously. In fact, the existence of such framing effects can be seen as an argument against the usefulness of all empirical work. We will regularly come back to it in the course of this book. Another interpretation, however, is that the theory is incomplete or even inadequate because it neglects crucial features of reality.

In Chapter 3 we will discuss in detail the seminal study by Yaari and Bar-Hillel (1984). Their respondents make a difference between 'needs' and 'tastes', which is not adequately captured by welfarist theories. These results have been influential in the theoretical debate on welfarism. In Chapter 4 we will see that respondents prefer different solutions in formally identical claims problems (where an amount of money is to be distributed over claimants whose individual claims sum up to a larger total), depending on whether the problem is formulated in terms of pensions or in terms of wage cuts (Bosmans and Schokkaert, 2009). This may be seen as an invitation to think about a 'metatheory' that would focus on defining in an abstract and general way which features of specific claims problems should play a role in determining which solutions are to be preferred.

An example of what this could lead to can be found in the theory of the measurement of inequality. A crucial element in the axiomatics of such measurement is the Pigou–Dalton principle, stating that a transfer of income from a richer to a poorer person which does not reverse the original income ranking of the two individuals, is inequality-decreasing. Empirical work has shown that a large fraction of the population does not accept this principle (Amiel and Cowell, 1999). A possible reaction would be to simply discard this evidence and argue that the population is not sufficiently clever to understand the intricacies of the distribution

problem. A more constructive reaction, however, is to 'take the empirical studies seriously' (Ebert, 2009) and analyse the formal implications
of alternative principles which are in line with (some of) the empirical
results and which are not less attractive from an *a priori* point of view.
In this context Ebert (2009) discussed a 'principle of concentration' (that
was originally introduced by Kolm, 1996), and Magdalou and Moyes
(2009) reinterpreted the idea of relative deprivation.

Note that in the examples given, the resulting theories should
not be seen as a mere *ex post* rationalization of the opinions of the
respondents. The empirical work does not suggest how to (re)formulate
the theory, though it may provide an indication that 'something' should
be reformulated. Its contribution is more modest: it is to suggest interesting puzzles and possibilities which would have remained un-
noticed without it. Let us repeat that the theorist in some cases might
prefer to interpret the empirical results as an indication of irrelevant
framing effects. Yet, this position should then also be argued for
convincingly. Such an argument can already yield useful theoretical
insights.

2.1.4 Empirical work as a complement

In some cases empirical results can be a necessary complement to the
theoretical work. This is obviously true if the ethical theory in itself
specifies a need for empirical information. An example is Roemer's
(1998) theory of equality of opportunity: this theory makes a distinction between 'effort', for which individuals are to be held responsible,
and 'circumstances' such as family background, for which they have to
be compensated. There is a whole philosophical debate about where to
draw the line between effort and circumstances (see, e.g., Fleurbaey,
2008), but in some of his writings Roemer states explicitly that this
boundary may be culture-dependent:

> Because the choice by society of these parameters cannot but be
> influenced by the physiological, psychological, and social theories
> of man that it has, the present proposal would implement

> different degrees of opportunity egalitarianism in different
> societies.　　　　　　　　　　　　　　　*(Roemer, 1993, p. 166)*

This is like an open invitation for empirical work on intercultural differences in the attribution of responsibility. The theory then offers a general and coherent framework which can be applied for any cut between effort and circumstances, while empirical work supplies the necessary information about where the boundary is drawn in different societies.

Empirical work may also be a necessary complement when trade-offs have to be made between different outcomes or different axioms. Suppose one agrees that both respect for individual rights and economic growth are important in poor societies. Yet, what to do in cases where these considerations come in conflict, e.g. if a policy would stimulate growth but violate individual rights, limiting the workers' right to strike, let us say? *A priori* ('objective') theories of well-being (such as the one by Nussbaum, 2000, 2006) might offer a framework for dealing with the resulting trade-offs, but even these theories often remain silent about the structure of relative weights and are therefore not very helpful in specific situations. Another approach, which is much more in line with the economic tradition, is to respect ('subjective') individual opinions and preferences about these trade-offs. In this latter approach, empirical work is needed to collect the necessary information about preferences (Gaertner, 2008). Note that the principle of 'respect for preferences' is an *a priori* principle, to be justified on philosophical grounds, and not on the basis of the opinions of citizens themselves. Yet, as soon as the *a priori* principle is accepted, empirical work may be needed to explore its implications in any specific case.

A related issue is the possible conflict between different desirable conditions or axioms. After theory has fully explored the logical links and possible contradictions between various axioms, it often ends up with a set of possible solutions to the problem, each satisfying some desirable axioms but violating other, possibly equally desirable, conditions. How then to choose between these different solutions, or: how to arbitrate between the various axioms? One could aim at a more comprehensive theory of how to arbitrate. The suggestion to look for a metatheory for choosing between different solutions to the claims problem goes in that direction. Yet empirical research may be useful in anticipation of this theory. And, here also, some theories might accept respect for individual preferences as a guiding principle. Later in this book, we will see examples where citizens seem to have clear opinions about trade-offs in situations where theory remains silent. In these cases, and at least until there is a more complete theory, empirical work can fill in the gaps that are (provisionally?) left open.

2.1.5 Empirical work as essential

Finally, there are arguments stating that the opinions held in society should be a constitutive factor of a good theory of justice. In his book on justice, Sen writes (2009, p. 44) that 'public reasoning is clearly an essential feature of objectivity in political and ethical beliefs ... In seeking resolution by public reasoning, there is clearly a strong case for not leaving out the perspectives and reasonings presented by anyone whose assessments are relevant, either because their interests are involved, or because their ways of thinking about these issues throw light on particular judgements – a light that might be missed in the absence of giving those perspectives an opportunity to be aired.'

A clear statement of this position is by Miller (1994). He starts from a distinction between what he calls the Platonic and the Aristotelian view. The Platonic approach points to the flaws in everyday beliefs about justice and then proposes a better (or the best) theory on the basis of a philosophical argumentation. As Miller notes, this presupposes (a) that there is a kind of 'objective' truth about justice, and (b) that this truth can be discovered by special methods of reasoning accessible only to philosophers (or even to one specific philosopher). These claims are difficult to defend. If there is an objective truth about justice to be discovered, why is the majority of people completely unable to do so (Miller, 1994, p. 178)? In contrast to this Platonic view, Miller describes the Aristotelian project, which consists in 'identifying and clarifying what people ordinarily mean when they invoke justice' (Miller, 1994, p. 178). This does not mean that justice coincides with the majority opinion. There are disagreements about justice, which can partly be explained by self-interest. Moreover, popular beliefs can be self-contradictory or rest on factual errors. Yet,

> the plausibility of the Aristotelian approach derives from the fact that, rather than resting upon esoteric epistemological claims, it seeks to correct common opinions using only methods of argument that common opinion itself endorses. *(Miller, 1994, p. 178)*

Miller (1994) relates this Aristotelian position to the work of Rawls (1971) and, more specifically, to the notion of 'reflective equilibrium'. In that approach one first formulates general principles and then confronts these general principles with one's considered judgments about specific practices or institutions. If there is a conflict, one either refines the general principles or one corrects the originally considered judgments until an equilibrium between the two has been reached. This process is an individual one, and therefore different persons may end up in a different reflective equilibrium. Yet, even in such an individualistic perspective, it is worth asking how a person can evaluate which of his primitive beliefs and intuitions should be treated as considered judgments. According to Miller, other people's beliefs are a crucial input in that exercise:

> Looking at what other people believe about justice, and in particular trying to understand when people disagree and what the grounds of their disagreement are, are integral to the process of deciding which of my own beliefs deserve to be taken as the fixed points of my considered judgments. *(Miller, 1994, p. 181)*

Miller goes even further in his 'Aristotelian' interpretation of Rawls. He points out that, according to Rawls, a valid theory of justice must be one which the citizens of a well-ordered society can justify to one another using only commonly accepted modes of argument. This goes much further than the argument described in subsection 2.1.1 that implementation of a theory of justice is only possible if the theory can be understood by the public at large. That was merely a feasibility argument. In Miller's Aristotelian view the possibility of justifying a theory of justice to other citizens is a precondition for it to be ethically acceptable.

In his later work, Rawls (1993) reinterprets the notion of decision-making in the original position by introducing a distinction between the 'rational' and the 'reasonable'. The latter implies that parties in the original position will not propose principles that are unacceptable to some people once the veil of ignorance is lifted. Yet, how can we find out what is 'reasonable' without invoking to some extent again the method of reflective equilibrium, 'moving back and forth between our particular beliefs about justice and the general principles that might be used to systematize them, always bearing in mind that these principles are meant to serve everybody in our society and must be publicly justifiable' (Miller, 1994, pp. 183–4)?[3] As Miller notes, in this interpretation of 'reasonable argumentation', the reflective equilibrium is no longer the equilibrium of one particular person, but must be seen as an interpersonal equilibrium among the beliefs of different members of a society.

Once one accepts that theories of justice reflect a kind of dialogue between the theorist and the public, empirical results by social scientists become immediately relevant. In fact, in their seminal paper, Yaari and Bar-Hillel (1984) give a justification for empirical social choice which is close to Miller's reasoning. They also start from the concept of reflective equilibrium. In their interpretation, economic theories of justice take the place of Rawls' principles, the answers by respondents in hypothetical specific choice situations take the place of Rawls' considered judgments. Although they are not explicit about this, they seem to support Miller's interpretation of the reflective equilibrium as an interpersonal equilibrium rather than a purely individualistic one.

A related perspective can be found in the practical, so-called 'Deweyan' approach proposed by Putnam (2008). He puts much less

---

[3] We will compare different versions of the original position in Chapter 3, in which we will also discuss the results of the empirical work in this regard.

emphasis on the search for a reflective equilibrium as an epistemological tool to derive an acceptable theory of justice and more emphasis on the importance of the democratic process as a way to discover what is reasonable. He claims that it is utopian to think that there will ever be consensus about the notion of justice. Therefore,

> The alternative we settle on in practice, instead of seeking the consent of 'all' or the consent of the 'reasonable', is to seek arguments that convince substantial majorities of citizens, arguments that may produce an 'overlapping consensus' ... Experts may not take formal votes, but if their policy recommendations are to be acceptable they must be arrived at by informed discussion that respects 'discourse ethics' and that tries to understand and make explicit the concerns of all affected.   (Putnam, 2008, p. 387)

This does *not* mean that justice simply coincides with the majority view in society. Yet it is less dangerous to accept the outcomes from a process of democratic discussions than to assent to the idiosyncratic view of one philosopher. Putnam therefore emphatically rejects the Platonic view and instead introduces a principle that he calls 'fallibilism' :

> What Deweyans possess is the 'democratic faith' that if we discuss things in a democratic manner, if we inquire carefully and if we *test* our proposals in an experimental spirit, and if we discuss the proposals and their tests thoroughly, then even if our conclusions will not always be right, nor always justified, nor always even reasonable – we are only human after all – still, we shall be right, we will be justified, we will be reasonable more often than if we relied on any foundational philosophical theory, and certainly more often than if we relied on any dogma, or any method fixed in advance of inquiry and held immune from revision in the course of inquiry.
> (Putnam, 2008, p. 387)

While Putnam is not explicit about the usefulness of empirical work on justice by social scientists, it is easy to argue that such work may be an interesting input to fuel democratic discussions that are the essential element in his Deweyan approach.

Views such as the ones of Miller and Yaari and Bar-Hillel certainly do not conflate social scientific research on justice with normative theory. A popular vote is not the ultimate justification of an ethical position. Opinions of the public are no more than an input (albeit a necessary one) into a broader philosophical debate aiming at a reflective equilibrium between theoretical principles and specific considered judgments. Putnam gives a larger weight to majority opinions, but also in his view there remains an essential tension between public opinion and normative thinking. Moreover, even if one accepts the crucial need for democratic legitimacy of a theory of justice, this principle of democratic legitimacy itself still has to be justified with independent philosophical arguments and cannot be justified by appeal to popular opinion (Swift, 1999). Therefore, the role of theoretical thinking remains essential. Yet, in these approaches, theoretical thinking should necessarily integrate in a critical way the findings of empirical work. The latter therefore is an essential ingredient into the normative debate.

2.1.6 Conclusion

In this section we have described five arguments to justify doing empirical social choice, in increasing order of the importance given to empirical results for the construction of a theory of justice. A following step could be to go even further than Putnam (2008) and take the position that the concept of justice has no meaning beyond its social construction, i.e. that its content can only and fully be derived on the basis of empirical research. We definitely do not want to go that far, as we are convinced that there is a role for theoretical thinking about justice – or, more explicitly stated, that majority opinions are not necessarily justified because they are supported by a majority. Critical reflection remains indispensable. However, we do believe that there is some value in the arguments sketched already. In fact, in order to support the conclusion that empirical research is useful, it is not necessary to accept all of these arguments fully. Each one of them on its own is sufficient to justify empirical social choice. This does not mean that it is not meaningful to think about the validity of each of these arguments. As a matter of fact, the weight given to each of them, will co-determine the specific methods that are used (or should be used) for the collection of the empirical data. Let us now turn to these methodological choices.

2.2 METHODOLOGICAL PRELIMINARIES

While it would be exaggerated to claim that there is consensus among scholars about how to set up the work in empirical social choice, the large bulk of the literature has some common features. In this section we will give a broad overview of these general characteristics. Most of them are a matter of principle and reflect the main purpose of this literature, i.e. to confront formalized social choice approaches with the opinions of lay respondents so as to derive normatively relevant information. Other characteristics are mainly dictated by practical considerations, however. It is useful to contrast these methodological choices with the arguments made in favour of empirical research in section 2.1.

2.2.1 Experiments or questionnaire studies?

The information used in empirical social choice is typically derived from the answers of respondents on questionnaires. Traditionally, questionnaire studies have not been very popular among economists. Quite often it has been argued, particularly by scholars who do experimental game theory in laboratories, that answers from questionnaires cannot be taken seriously because these answers have no monetary consequences at all for those who evaluate. This criticism has much force if the purpose of the empirical investigation is to *predict* actual behaviour. Actual behaviour will normally not be driven primarily by normative considerations, but will reflect a mixture of self-interest, norms and the desire to make a good impression on the experimenter. A questionnaire study may then reveal only 'socially desirable' answers and it would indeed be inappropriate to derive any behavioural predictions from it, as the real-world incentives are very different from the incentives in the questionnaire environment.[4] Therefore, predicting behaviour is not what the work in empirical social choice focuses on. The aim of this research is to derive information about norms. In that case, one can turn the argument around and say that the subjects should be genuinely interested in the underlying issues which the experimenter wishes to study, and not primarily in the sum of money they can bring home after the experiment. In a study about norms, we do not want the subjects to be guided by self-interested considerations. Questionnaire studies without monetary payments are then a natural approach. The hypothesis that respondents in questionnaire–experimental situations without monetary payments would tend to supply 'any' answer is based on a strange view of human behaviour. It may be true that, if the questions are too difficult, some of the respondents may not exert the necessary intellectual effort to answer carefully (which would also happen in game-theory-based laboratory investigations, we believe). But if the intellectual effort is not too demanding, why would respondents lie? In any case, as we will see, the response patterns in the questionnaire studies are clear, understandable and far from random.

While we will focus in this book on questionnaire studies, we will make an exception for one branch of experimental work. This branch draws its inspiration from an approach in political philosophy and social choice that is directly related to the distinction between self-interested and ethically motivated decisions, i.e. that of the so-called 'veil of ignorance' (VOI, or original position). Rawls (1971) and Harsanyi (1955) have popularized the idea that subjects are revealing their ethical preferences when they take rational self-interested decisions in a hypothetical situation in which they do not know their own relative position in society. Some experimental work has tried to make this hypothetical position operational in a laboratory environment. We will discuss this

---

[4] Even this point is not generally accepted among game theorists. Rubinstein (1999) said, after having done questionnaire–experimental studies in an introductory course on game theory, that he would like to stress his doubts 'as to the necessity of laboratory conditions and the use of real money in experimental game theory'.

work in more depth in Chapter 3, where we will also compare its results with those obtained from questionnaire studies on the same topic.

2.2.2 A quasi-experimental approach: direct versus indirect testing of axioms

An obvious possibility to test for the empirical acceptance of theoretical ideas or axioms would be to formulate direct questions about them, e.g. 'Is it just that differences in natural talent lead to differences in income?', or: 'Should educational funding give priority to the needs of a handicapped person, whatever the number of intelligent children that get less as a result of the policy?' Such direct questions force the respondents to think in an abstract way about general principles concerning problems that are relatively new to them. It is then hard to avoid framing effects, i.e. the formulation of the questions may have a strong influence on the answers by the respondents. For this reason, the largest part of the literature has followed another route. The respondents are confronted with specific stories that are related to real-world situations, and are then asked to give their opinion about what is a just (or optimal) distribution in that specific situation.[5] Sometimes they get a series of possible options from which they can choose. Some of these correspond to theoretical solutions while others are unrelated to any theoretical concept. The relative popularity of the various options then offers an indirect way to test different axioms or solution concepts. Confronting respondents with specific stories is less suggestive than formulating abstract principles, and brings us closer to their own original ethical intuitions. Moreover, the formulation of specific cases fits very well the 'reflective equilibrium' approach described in section 2.1. The answers to the specific cases capture the judgments and intuitions of the respondents, which have to be confronted with the theoretical axioms or solutions that represent the underlying philosophical principles.

---

[5] The method is closely related to the vignette studies on just income differences that have been used by sociologists (see, e.g., Alves and Rossi, 1978).

Often the method has been refined by presenting different variants of the same story to different (randomly selected) samples of subjects. The different variants are used to manipulate those features of the situation that are relevant from a theoretical point of view. In this quasi-experimental setup, differences in the response patterns between the variants can only be ascribed to the differences in their formulation – i.e. to the manipulated theoretical features – since everything else is kept constant. The danger of suggesting or provoking socially desirable answers is then even less, as all individual respondents are confronted with only one variant of the story and are not aware of what is being 'tested' in the study. Many examples of this approach will be discussed in the following chapters.

While this quasi-experimental approach has clear advantages, it has also its limitations. In fact, if one questionnaire contained all the relevant variants of one and the same story, one would force the respondents to compare the variants and to think about the differences. This would yield some insights into their reasoned opinions, rather than into their original ethical intuitions. One could even go further. One could in a first round ask respondents simple questions revealing their original intuitions, and afterwards give them additional information about the implications of their choices or explicitly confront their answers with the position that the theory would take.[6] There is a clear trade-off here. The simple quasi-experimental setup allows us to remain close to the original ethical intuitions of the respondents – but these may be very primitive. If we force the respondents to think more explicitly, we will get more sophisticated answers. However, these answers may be heavily influenced by the setup of the questionnaire, and hence by the structure of the dominant theory. This is especially true if the respondents had no strong opinions before they were confronted with the questionnaire.

---

[6] Something similar is done in the work by Amiel and Cowell (1999) on economic inequality. They first ask the respondents to evaluate numerical income vectors, and then confront them with a verbal formulation of the relevant axioms. After the verbal part, respondents can return and change their answers on the numerical questions if they want to. It turns out, however, that only a small minority of respondents revises their original answers.

The method to be followed will therefore necessarily depend on what the main objectives of the study are.

2.2.3 Representative versus student samples

While questionnaire studies in sociology and psychology usually work with representative surveys, most studies in empirical social choice use student samples. Although this choice is not a matter of principle and is mainly explained by the easy availability of students, it has an obvious advantage. Students can be expected to understand rather complicated questions, which could not be introduced easily in a representative survey. As mentioned before, random answers or refusals to answer are possible if the intellectual effort demanded from the respondents is too large. In fact, setting up a quasi-experimental study with representative samples is possible but could be rather costly. On the other hand, the lack of representativeness is an obvious disadvantage for some purposes.[7] There is again a trade-off here.

We can make this trade-off more explicit by linking it to the main arguments that were described in section 2.1 (see Table 2.1). It is obvious that the use of representative samples is to be preferred if one wants to check whether the theoretical approach is supported by different groups in society, or if one wants to get a better insight into social biases

Table 2.1. *Representative versus student samples*

Representative samples	Student samples
Acceptance of axioms by society	Students as future decision-makers
Awareness of biases	Suggesting interesting questions
Intercultural differences	Trade-offs between axioms
'Aristotelian' approach	

[7] Schokkaert and Capeau (1991) show that the response pattern of students is different from that of their parents.

and intercultural differences. In some situations, however, one might prefer to focus on non-representative groups. As an example, consider the fact that most situations in empirical social choice are intimately related to issues in economic or social policy. In order to check the political feasibility of different solutions, it can then be interesting to focus on the decision-makers in this domain and to investigate what their dominant values are. From this perspective, students are an interesting subgroup of the population, as they may be seen as the future economic and political elite of the country. Representative samples are definitely needed if one takes the Aristotelian approach seriously. On the other hand, the fact that one can probably formulate more difficult questions with student samples may be a decisive advantage if one wants to apply the quasi-experimental approach to discover new puzzles or to get a better insight into the trade-offs between different axioms. To some extent, the popularity of student samples in earlier work may reflect the fact that these latter objectives were the most important for the researchers involved. In any case, whatever the original interest of the researchers, the limitations of using student samples should not be neglected. It would certainly be interesting to have more questionnaire studies with representative samples.

2.2.4 Experienced versus inexperienced respondents

Should respondents be acquainted with an underlying theory? Two points of view are possible here. One is that ethical thinking is necessarily complicated and that one cannot expect interesting information to be derived from the answers of uninformed and possibly even uninterested respondents. In this view, an elementary insight into the essentials of the theory is needed before one can answer sufficiently interesting questions in a meaningful way. The opposite point of view states that respondents should not be acquainted with the theory, because in that case they would already be heavily influenced by the considerations which we want to submit to empirical scrutiny. If the purpose of the empirical research is to detect the biases or the one-sidedness in the existing approaches, it does not make much sense to use respondents that have already been biased in the same direction. The problem is even worse when working with students, because they might see the experiment as a test to check whether they really understood the theory behind the questions, with the consequence that the whole study may turn into an exam or an IQ test. This is clearly not what we are looking for.

The work in empirical social choice has taken the second perspective. Most studies are careful in pointing out that the respondents involved were not acquainted with the theory before the experiment started. Yet it is obvious that the first perspective can also be defended and that the two approaches reflect different views on the use of empirical results for normative thinking. This issue is closely related to the choice between the different ways of setting up the questionnaire, discussed in subsection 2.2.2. If one takes seriously the idea of a dialogue between empirical results and theoretical principles, it would definitely be interesting to experiment with the dynamic setup that has been described there. One then starts with unexperienced respondents to get, in a first round, information about their original judgments. In the next round, however, the questionnaire could point out possible incoherences in these original judgments, or explicitly draw attention to the (possibly conflicting) proposals of different theories. One would then to some extent 'educate' the respondents in the course of the experiment and investigate whether they are sensitive to the arguments used by the various theories. Setting up such a dynamic study would not be a trivial exercise; but it could be highly rewarding.

2.2.5 Formulation and framing issues

Clearly, the most important aspect in a questionnaire study is the formulation of the questions. There is an essential difference between asking about 'justice' and asking about 'optimality', and maximizing social welfare does not necessarily lead to the same policy prescriptions as minimizing inequality. Moreover, the exact phrasing in the description of the situation may matter a lot. An extra word (e.g. 'luckily' or 'unfortunately', 'healthy' or 'unhealthy', 'dangerous' or 'safe') can easily achieve manipulative force which the researcher should try to avoid.

It is essential to keep these differences in mind when interpreting the results. That is why we will be careful in the following chapters always to include the exact wording of the questions.

An even more basic challenge is the framing problem, described first by Tversky and Kahneman (1981). They have shown that, in some circumstances, respondents may give different answers to different variants of a choice problem, even if the underlying situation and the basic outcomes are *exactly the same* under all these variants. A prominent example of this phenomenon occurs when a certain situation has positive and negative features. It is then often the case that framing in positive terms will elicit different reactions than framing in negative terms. The interpretation of the framing problem in the normative context of empirical social choice is not always straightforward, however, and it may be argued that in some cases the 'framing' is not an artefact of the method but, rather, a normatively essential feature of the situation. As noted before, we will encounter in the following chapters many examples of context-dependence of justice opinions, even if there is no reason for such context-dependence in the dominant theories. Is this a framing effect or rather an indication that the underlying theory is incomplete? Note, moreover, that even if the starting positions and the final outcomes in two variants are exactly the same, it is very possible that respondents will attach some weight to the procedure by which these outcomes were reached. We will return to these issues later in this book.

2.3 CONCLUSION

Empirical social choice is not a substitute for theoretical social choice, but it can be a useful or even indispensable complement. We favour the interpretation in which the purpose of social choice is to reach a balance between, on the one hand, theoretical principles as reflected in axioms and solution concepts and, on the other hand, judgments and ethical intuitions in specific situations. In this interpretation the quasi-experimental approach is especially appropriate. However, both less and more ambitious interpretations of the role of empirical research can also be defended, and the methodological choices should be adapted to the specific objectives of the researcher. Some of the existing research lacks this methodological awareness. We will return to these broader issues in the final Chapter 6.

3 Traditional questions in social choice

Social choice theory really took off with Arrow's seminal impossibility theorem (Arrow, 1951, 1963). This statement in no way wishes to belittle the great achievements and insights gained by de Borda, Condorcet, and others several centuries ago. Arrow formulated the problem of social choice in a very abstract setting.[1] Consider a set of social states which has to be ranked by the social planner. Suppose the only information available to construct this social ranking consists of the ordinal preferences of the individuals over the social states. How can these individual rankings be mapped into a social ranking? Arrow showed that there does not exist an aggregation procedure satisfying a set of reasonably looking axioms on a universal domain of individual preferences.

This impossibility theorem spawned a large literature, in both voting theory and in welfare economics. One influential strand of this literature built further on the insight that Arrow's setup restricted the available information for the planner to ordinal and interpersonally non-comparable individual utilities. It is not surprising that one cannot easily rank different distributions if interpersonal comparability is banned.[2] The so-called 'informational' approach to social choice (d'Aspremont and Gevers, 1977; Roberts, 1980; Sen, 1970) showed that introducing various forms of interpersonal comparability of utility made it possible to escape from Arrow's impossibility deadlock and to formulate so-called 'welfarist' social objective functions. The use of

---

[1] A rigorous but accessible introduction to social choice theory can be found in Gaertner (2009).

[2] Recent developments in the theory of fair allocation have shown that, even using only ordinal preferences without interpersonal comparability, there are escape routes out of the impossibility impasse (Fleurbaey and Maniquet, 2008; Fleurbaey and Mongin, 2005).

the term 'welfarist' has recently become ambiguous, because it has received many different connotations (Fleurbaey, 2003), but its original meaning was clear: an approach is called 'welfarist' if only the individual subjective utilities matter for the evaluation of social states. Welfarism does allow for different attitudes towards distribution. In the specific case of utilitarianism, which defines the social objective as the simple sum of the utilities of all individuals in society, the inequality aversion is equal to zero. The economic reinterpretation of Rawls' (1971) difference principle, in which the social objective is to maximize the welfare level of the worst-off in society, is also welfarist with an inequality aversion equal to infinity. In addition, applied work in public economics has popularized intermediate forms of concave social welfare functions with an inequality aversion between zero and infinity (see, e.g., Atkinson, 1970).

There has been a lively debate in the literature about the pros and cons of these different social welfare functions. Most attention has been given to the two polar cases of utilitarianism and Rawlsian maximin (or leximin, the lexicographic extension of maximin). It has been argued that the former is ethically unacceptable because it is unconcerned about the distribution of utilities, and that the latter (even in its leximin form) is too extreme in its exclusive focus on the worst-off. The discussion got a methodological twist as both the utilitarians (mainly inspired by Harsanyi, 1953, 1955, 1978) and Rawls (1971) used the concept of an original position behind a veil of ignorance, and yet the decision rules they derived were very different. While this discussion in economics was largely cast in welfarist terms, Rawls himself strongly objected to welfarism and proposed to compare people's positions in terms of the more objective concept of 'primary goods' such as basic liberties, opportunities, income and wealth. Partly inspired by this Rawlsian position, the debate in welfare economics soon went beyond the comparison of different social welfare functions to tackle the basic assumption of welfarism itself (Sen, 1979, 1980; Sen and Williams, 1982). The idea that the only information needed to evaluate social states is information about the subjective utilities of the individuals has come under heavy attack. It has been argued that information about the underlying causes of the differences in subjective welfare, or information about other aspects of social states (such as respect for individual rights), cannot be discarded as irrelevant.

The empirical social choice literature has contributed to the debate in a number of ways. Its basic methodology of comparing different variants of the same base situation is particularly well suited to check the acceptance of informational restrictions. More specifically, the seminal paper in empirical social choice (Yaari and Bar-Hillel, 1984) formulated in a clever way three different situations, which are formally identical from a welfarist perspective, but differ from each other with respect to situational features that should not influence the evaluation from a welfarist perspective. If respondents react differently to these different situations this can be seen as support for the critique on welfarism. We will summarize this work in section 3.1. We then go into different aspects of the comparison between utilitarianism and maximin. In section 3.2 we discuss some studies that checked whether the Rawlsian assumption of absolute priority for the worst-off is accepted by the population. In sections 3.3 and 3.4 we look at the relevance and the implications of the veil of ignorance. Finally, in section 3.5 we consider the Pareto principle. Section 3.6 concludes. Non-welfarist approaches to social choice will be discussed in Chapter 4.

3.1 WELFARISM: NEEDS, TASTES AND BELIEFS

Yaari and Bar-Hillel (1984) used the quasi-experimental approach described in Chapter 2 to investigate the empirical acceptance of welfarism. As mentioned already, they presented three variants of the same situation to different random samples of young applicants for admission to the Hebrew University of Jerusalem in the years 1978–80. In each case respondents were asked to divide a bundle of goods between two persons in what they considered to be a 'just' way. Five different distributions were suggested, corresponding to different theoretical concepts. These included utilitarianism and maximin, but also some solutions from bargaining theory. We will mainly focus on the results concerning utilitarianism and maximin.

The first variant ran as follows:

Q 3.1: A shipment containing 12 grapefruit and 12 avocados is to be distributed between Jones and Smith. The following information is given, and is known also to the two recipients:

- Doctors have determined that Jones's metabolism is such that his body derives 100 milligrammes of vitamin F from each grapefruit consumed, while it derives no vitamin F whatsoever from an avocado.
- Doctors have also determined that Smith's metabolism is such that his body derives 50 milligrammes of vitamin F from each grapefruit consumed and also from each avocado consumed.
- Both persons, Jones and Smith, are interested in the consumption of grapefruit and/or avocados only insofar as such consumption provides vitamin F – and the more the better. All the other traits of the two fruits (such as taste, calorie content, etc.) are of no consequence to them.
- No trades can be made after the division takes place.

How should the fruits be divided between Jones and Smith, if the division is to be just?[3]

This problem of dividing grapefruit and avocados can be expressed more succinctly or more technically in the following way. Let ω be the bundle of fruits to be divided between Jones and Smith so that we have $\omega = (12, 12)$. Jones and Smith have different abilities to metabolize the fruits into vitamins. Therefore, we shall write $u_J(g, a) = 100g$ for Jones

---

[3] In fact, there were two different versions of Q 3.1. One version asked the students to mark which of the five distributions *they* considered as the most just. The other version asked the respondents to assess how Jones and Smith would divide the shipment, 'on the assumption that both recipients are committed to looking for a just division' (Yaari and Bar-Hillel, 1984, p. 10, n. 10). The authors report that differences between the distributions of responses to these two versions were negligible. We only report the results for the first version.

and $u_S(g, a) = 50g + 50a$ for Smith, with g and a being quantities of grapefruit and avocados, respectively. The functions u_J and u_S can be interpreted as biological functions, but in this *ceteris paribus* setting they can also be viewed as the utility functions of the two persons, since both Jones and Smith care only about their consumption of vitamin F. Moreover, these functions can be interpreted as cardinal utility functions with the property that the units of measurement (milligrammes of vitamin) are comparable across the individuals. Human beings certainly do not control their ability to metabolize fruits into vitamins and, moreover, the take-up of vitamins is necessary to remain healthy. The first variant can therefore be seen as an example of different *needs*. In the second variant, presented to a different sample of students, the situation was rewritten in such a way that the underlying issue was not needs but rather *subjective tastes*. More specifically, Jones and Smith now differ in their tastes for grapefruit and avocados which immediately affects their willingness-to-pay. Consider the following situation:

> **Q 3.2**: A shipment containing 12 grapefruit and 12 avocados is to be distributed between Jones and Smith. The following information is given, and is known also to the two recipients:
>
> - Jones likes grapefruit very much, and is willing to buy any number of them, provided that the price does not exceed $1.00 per pound. He detests avocados, so he never buys them.
> - Smith likes grapefruit and avocados equally well, and is willing to buy both grapefruit and avocados in any number, provided that the price does not exceed $0.50 per pound.
> - Jones and Smith are in the same income-tax bracket.
> - No trades can be made after the division takes place.
>
> How should the fruits be divided between Jones and Smith, if the division is to be just?

It is important to notice that this situation can be formalized in *exactly* the same way as the problem of Q 3.1. The two functions u_J and u_S now describe the willingness-to-pay of the two individuals who are in the same income-tax bracket. Therefore the information that is conveyed is information about the tastes of Jones and Smith, while previously the two functions contained information about their respective needs. However, from the standpoint of welfarism, these differences should only matter if they resulted in different utility information. Other information, such as the interpretation of the individuals' utilities, should be irrelevant. Since the utility information is identical in situations Q 3.1 and Q 3.2, a 'welfarist respondent' should take the same decision in both cases.

Let us now turn to the third variant in Yaari and Bar–Hillel (1984):

Q 3.3: A shipment containing 12 grapefruit and 12 avocados is to be distributed between Jones and Smith. The following information is given, and is known also to the two recipients:

- Jones believes that each grapefruit contains 100 milligrammes of vitamin F and that an avocado does not contain vitamin F at all.
- Smith believes that a grapefruit and an avocado each contains 50 milligrammes of vitamin F.
- Information regarding the true vitamin contents of the fruits is not available.
- Both persons, Jones and Smith, are interested in the consumption of grapefruit and/or avocados only insofar as such consumption provides vitamin F – and the more, the better. All the other traits of the two fruits (such as taste, calorie content, etc.) are of no consequence to them.
- No trades can be made after the division takes place.

How should the fruits be divided between Jones and Smith, if the division is to be just?

In formal terms, we have again the same structure as in the two earlier variants. There is an initial endowment $\omega = (12, 12)$ and there are the two utility functions $u_J(g, a) = 100g$ and $u_S(g, a) = 50g + 50a$. The only twist is that the utility functions are now describing *beliefs* about the vitamin contents of grapefruit and avocados rather than the 'objective' knowledge of medical doctors.

Table 3.1. *Welfarism: Yaari and Bar-Hillel (1984)*

Distribution (1)	Needs ($n = 163$) % of respondents (2)	Tastes ($n = 122$) % of respondents (3)	Beliefs ($n = 145$) % of respondents (4)
J: 6,6; S: 6,6	8	9	34
J: 6,0; S: 6,12	0	4	4
J: 8,0; S: 4,12	82	28	51
J: 9,0; S: 3,12	8	24	4
J: 12,0; S: 0,12	2	35	7

How did the students divide the given bundle of 12 grapefruit and 12 avocados between Jones and Smith in these three cases? The results are given in Table 3.1, where (J: 9,0; S: 3,12), for example, means that Jones gets 9 grapefruit and no avocados, while Smith receives 3 grapefruit and 12 avocados. Column (2) refers to Q 3.1, column (3) to Q 3.2, column (4) to Q 3.3. In all three variants the maximin criterion advocates an equal distribution of utilities (interpreted differently, of course, in the three variants), i.e. the distribution (J: 8,0; S: 4,12), while utilitarianism, maximizing the sum of utilities, advocates (J: 12,0; S: 0,12).[4]

Let us focus first on a comparison of the 'needs' and 'tastes' cases. In both, strict equality of fruit is supported only by a minority. In fact, equal split of the number of fruit is Pareto-inefficient. In the case of 'needs' (column (2)), the Rawlsian solution (J: 8,0; S: 4,12), i.e. a division which takes account of differing degrees of metabolic efficiency and yields an equal amount of vitamins, if possible, is favoured by a large majority. In the 'tastes' case (column (3)), the distribution of answers is

---

[4] One cannot immediately derive from the answers whether respondents follow the maximin or the utilitarian criterion, however. Actually, the distribution (J: 8,0; S: 4,12) is not only 'supported' by the Rawlsian criterion, but also, e.g., by bargaining from zero according to the solution of Kalai and Smorodinsky (1975).

quite different (the authors mention that under a χ^2 test, the difference between the distributions is significant at the 1% level). Although in the latter case, the distribution (J: 8,0; S: 4,12) still receives a relatively high percentage of support, this support is much less than under Q 3.1, and the most popular solution has now become (J: 12,0; S: 0,12) which is advocated, as stated before, by utilitarianism. It is interesting to see that the more egalitarian maximin criterion loses its attractiveness if we move from a situation in terms of needs to a situation in terms of tastes, while the more efficiency-oriented utilitarian criterion gains popularity. More important, however, than the specific direction of the differences, is the plain and simple fact that there are differences. As noted before, for a welfarist the distinction between needs and tastes is irrelevant, and there should have been no differences. Welfarism seems to be decisively rejected for the student samples of Yaari and Bar-Hillel.

We now turn to beliefs. Somewhat more than half of the respondents pick again (J: 8,0; S: 4,12). These respondents honour the beliefs of the two agents and clearly wish that there be an equal amount of vitamin obtained by the two, each according to his own beliefs. Actually, this solution yields the highest equal-vitamin outcome possible. While this division also received fairly strong support in the 'tastes' case, other solutions that were popular in the latter case (such as the division (J: 9,0; S: 3,12) or the utilitarian solution (J: 12,0; S: 0,12)) are hardly chosen in the case of beliefs. Although subjective beliefs and tastes *a priori* seem to be closely related, for the respondents they apparently represent different categories.

The most striking observation in the beliefs case is the relative popularity of the equal split solution (J: 6,6; S: 6,6). While equal split was chosen by only a few respondents in Q 3.1 and Q 3.2, in the case of beliefs it is picked by one-third of the respondents. Apparently, while subjective statements about tastes (and the willingness-to-pay as an expression of such statements) are taken seriously, this is much less true for subjective beliefs. Can equal split be considered a just distribution? Clearly not, if one takes the beliefs of the two persons seriously. For both of them, given their beliefs, the distributions (J: 8,0; S:4,12) and (J: 9,0; S: 3,12) would be improvements over equal split. If beliefs are subjective 'utility' statements, then ignoring these statements violates consumer sovereignty. Indeed, Bar-Hillel and Yaari argue that maintaining an equal-split distribution could be viewed as an act of coercion, going against the self-perceived interests of the persons involved. If the beliefs, however, were nothing else but subjective feelings without any firm grounds, it could be deemed better to decide in favour of an equal split and find out at a later stage what the true vitamin contents are. In sharp contrast to Q 3.1, there is no 'real' difference between the two individuals, except for their beliefs. A risk-averse individual or a person who is sceptical towards personal beliefs may argue that possible mistakes are kept 'small' with an equal split.[5] Moreover, Yaari and Bar-Hillel develop an interesting counter-argument against the assertion that imposing equal split implies coercion. If Jones were a moral person, he should object to a move from equal split to (J: 9,0; S: 3,12), for example. While such a move would undoubtedly be beneficial for him, given his beliefs, the same move would reduce Smith's vitamin intake from 600 to 300. Likewise if Smith were a moral person, he should also object to a move from equal split to (J: 9,0; S: 3,12), since this change would reduce Jones' vitamin consumption from 600 to 450, given Smith's beliefs. This raises the deeper question whether one has a moral obligation to protect others from their, as one thinks, wrong beliefs.

In any case, the most important finding of Yaari and Bar-Hillel (1984) is that the three distribution problems are viewed as very different from one another by the respondents although, as we have indicated, their mathematical formulations in terms of individual utility functions are the same. This can be seen as a strong argument against welfarism. As noted in Chapter 2, one may take the position that

---

[5] In fact, the formulation of Q 3.3 suggests that the beliefs of Jones and Smith are contradictory and therefore cannot both be correct. 'Mistakes' are then unavoidable and there is no *a priori* reason to prefer the beliefs of one of the two individuals over those of the other.

empirical regularities as such do not offer an argument to discard ethical theories. However, in this case, the relevance of the distinction between needs, tastes and subjective beliefs seems to be deeply rooted in our moral intuitions.[6] Moreover, the results of the Yaari and Bar-Hillel (1984) questionnaire study are well in line with recent philosophical arguments against welfarism. One possible interpretation of their results is that individuals cannot be held responsible for their biological needs, but should not be compensated for their subjective tastes. We will return to the issue of responsibility in Chapter 4.

3.2 THE RAWLSIAN EQUITY AXIOM

We have seen that in the case of needs, respondents tend to favour the allocation proposed by the maximin criterion. This is in line with the Rawlsian difference principle, stating that economic and social inequalities be arranged such that they are to the greatest benefit of the least advantaged members of society. It is well known that this implies that an infinitesimal improvement of the welfare of the worst-off is enough to compensate for extremely large decreases in the welfare of the better-off as long as they still remain better off. Maximin corresponds to an infinite inequality aversion. However, the results in section 3.1 are not sufficient to see whether respondents want to go that far. In the described case, maximin boiled down to an equal distribution of vitamins without implying an extremely unequal distribution of the fruit. Do respondents indeed accept the difference principle in its pure (extreme) form? In their specific setting, Yaari and Bar-Hillel (1984) reformulate the question as follows: 'How long' or to what extent would the respondents be willing to compensate Smith for any further deterioration in his metabolism if, simultaneously, Jones's share of grapefruit is relentlessly cut down? They suggest that from a certain point onwards this process runs the risk of becoming morally unsound. To test for the acceptance of this idea, the authors conceived

---

[6] Evans (1984) gives the following illustrative example: 'The statement "Oh Lord, I need a Mercedes-Benz!" is a joke. "Oh Lord, I need a coronary artery by-pass graft!" is not'.

yet two additional variants of the distribution problem formulated in
Q 3.1. Everything remains the same, but the third paragraph is sub-
stituted by

> **Q 3.4**: Doctors have also determined that Smith's metabolism is
> such that his body derives 20 milligrammes of vitamin F from each
> grapefruit consumed and also from each avocado consumed.

This implies that Smith's metabolism is less effective than originally.
In technical terms, the problem now reads:

$$38; \omega = (12, 12);$$
$$38; u_J(g, a) = 100g;$$
$$38; u_S(g, a) = 20g + 20a.$$

Going even further, they also formulate

> **Q 3.5**: Doctors have also determined that Smith's metabolism is
> such that his body derives 9.1 milligrammes of vitamin F from each
> grapefruit and also from each avocado consumed.

In technical terms, the situation now looks as follows:

$$38; \omega = (12, 12);$$
$$38; u_J(g, a) = 100g;$$
$$38; u_S(g, a) = 9.1g + 9.1a.$$

In each of these variants, maximin compensates Smith for the deterioration in his metabolism and advocates an equal distribution of vitamin F. This implies an ever more unequal distribution of the fruit.
While the maximin criterion supported (J: 8,0; S: 4,12) in Q 3.1, it
advocates (J: 4,0; S: 8,12) in the new question Q 3.4 and the extremely
unequal distribution of the fruit (J: 2,0; S: 10,12) in Q 3.5. Note that, as a
result of the decrease in efficiency of Smith's metabolism, the vitamin
intake for Jones declines from 800 to 400 and even 200 in Q 3.5.
Moreover, also from the viewpoint of efficiency, an eyebrow could be
raised. The distributions (J: 4,0; S: 8,12) and, *a fortiori*, (J: 2,0; S: 10,12)

Table 3.2. *Decreasing the effectiveness of Smith's metabolism*

Distribution (1)	Q 3.1 ($n = 163$) % of respondents (2)	Q 3.4 ($n = 146$) % of respondents (3)	Q 3.5 ($n = 52$) % of respondents (4)
J: 6,6; S: 6,6	8	4	17
J: 2,0; S: 10,12	–	–	38
J: 4,0; S: 8,12	0	82	–
J: 6,0; S: 6,12	–	4	27
J: 8,0; S: 4,12	82	7	6
J: 1,0; S: 3,12	8	–	–
J: 12,0; S: 0,12	2	3	12

considerably diminish the combined amount of vitamin intake from the available fruit.

The results for these variants are shown in Table 3.2. Needless to say, the respondents were different for the different variants. The students' 'vote' in favour of a maximin-supported division in Q 3.4 is amazing, in both absolute terms and in relation to the other proposals. Yaari and Bar-Hillel remark that one might, perhaps, have expected this, given the fact that the problem presented to the students isolated the issue of needs and, furthermore, needs were readily quantifiable. However, even under these conditions, further decreasing the efficiency of Smith's metabolism (in Q 3.5) leads to a large loss of the attractiveness of maximin. It still receives the largest number of responses but other proposals such as (J: 6,0; S: 6,12) and even equal split which is totally insensitive to 'the story behind' gain much more support than before. Would maximin be abandoned altogether if Smith's metabolic deficiency were enhanced even further? We do not know. Yaari and Bar-Hillel's investigation, however, indicates that the criterion of equalizing the satisfaction of needs which maximin requires in the present case may at some point collide with the moral intuitions of their respondents.

Table 3.3. *Decreasing Smith's willingness-to-pay*

Distribution (1)	Q 3.2 (n = 122) % of respondents (2)	Q 3.6 (n = 102) % of respondents (3)
J: 6,6; S: 6,6	9	12
J: 4,0; S: 8,12	–	6
J: 6,0; S: 6,12	4	7
J: 8,0; S: 4,12	28	6
J: 9,0; S: 3,12	24	–
J: 12,0; S: 0,12	35	47

Yaari and Bar-Hillel (1984) also tested the degree of inequality aversion in a version of the tastes' case. In that variant they alter Smith's willingness to pay in Q 3.2 in such a way that the technical description becomes identical to the one in problem Q 3.4. The third paragraph then reads:

> **Q 3.6**: Smith likes grapefruit and avocado equally well, and is willing to buy both grapefruit and avocado in any number, provided that the price does not exceed $0.20 per pound.

The results are given in column (3) of Table 3.3, where column (2) repeats the results for Q 3.2 (the 'tastes' column (3) in Table 3.1) for the sake of comparison. The outcome is very interesting. While a very large number of students wanted to compensate Smith for the setback in his metabolism in situation Q 3.4 (cutting Jones's share simultaneously), nothing of this kind happens in the case of tastes. The considerable decline in responses consistent with maximin (from 28% in Q 3.2 to 6% in Q 3.6) and the clear increase in answers consistent with utilitarianism (from 35% in Q 3.2 to 47% in Q 3.6) rather appear to penalize Smith for a drop in his willingness-to-pay. This confirms again that, for Israeli students, needs and tastes have to be treated very differently from the point of view of justice.

The results by Yaari and Bar-Hillel suggest that an infinite inequality aversion is too extreme for their respondents, even in the case of differences in needs. Although this raises questions concerning the acceptability of the maximin criterion, in their analysis the proposed divisions cannot be linked unambiguously to theoretical solution concepts. Given the purpose of empirical social choice, as described in Chapter 2, it would be more interesting to insert the question on the acceptance of the Rawlsian difference principle in a coherent axiomatic structure. This effort was pursued in a series of studies by Gaertner and his collaborators (Gaertner, 1992; Gaertner and Jungeilges, 2002; Gaertner and Schwettmann, 2007; Gaertner, et al. 2001). In these studies, the focus is on the so-called 'equity axiom' that is fundamental for Rawls' second principle of justice (see Gaertner, 2009). The equity axiom formulated by d'Aspremont and Gevers (1977), Hammond (1976) and Sen (1973), among others, makes a particular demand for a society of only two individuals or, more generally, for a society where only two individuals are affected by a change from one policy to another. Let there be two policies, x and y. We postulate that person 1 prefers x to y, person 2 prefers y to x, and independently of whether x or y will eventually be the social outcome, person 2 is always better-off than person 1. In this situation, the equity axiom requires x to be socially preferred to y. Since this axiom is closely related to the Rawlsian difference principle, it is very instructive to check whether it is followed by individual respondents. Moreover, we would like to know whether those who fulfil the axiom follow it *unconditionally*, i.e., focus always exclusively on the worst-off members of society, even if this leads to an increasing loss of efficiency. This second step is closely related to the variants within the Yaari and Bar-Hillel investigation, where Smith's metabolism becomes poorer and poorer.

Gaertner (1992) made the following suggestion to test for the acceptance of the equity axiom. Consider the subsequent two-person profile of so–called extended orderings $\tilde{R}_i, i \in \{1,2\}$, that we shall denote by E^1.

$$38; \tilde{R}_1: (y,2)(x,2)(x,1)(y,1),$$
$$38; \tilde{R}_2: (y,2)(x,2)(x,1)(y,1).$$

These lines should be read as follows. Both individuals agree that it is best to be person 2 under policy y. This is deemed better than being person 2 under policy x. This, again, is better than being person 1 under policy x which is better than being person 1 under policy y. The reader should verify that this two-person profile mirrors the structure of the equity axiom just stated. Both persons diverge in their evaluations of policies x and y as far as *their own position* is concerned, but they agree that it is person 2 who is always better-off.

According to the equity axiom, x will be declared as preferable to y. We shall now enlarge this basic profile by adding the extended orderings of persons 3, 4, ..., thereby preserving the structure of E^1. E^2, for example, is:

$$\tilde{R}_1: (y,3)(x,3)(y,2)(x,2)(x,1)(y,1), \quad 38;$$
$$\tilde{R}_2: (y,3)(x,3)(y,2)(x,2)(x,1)(y,1), \quad 38;$$
$$\tilde{R}_3: (y,3)(x,3)(y,2)(x,2)(x,1)(y,1). \quad 38;$$

We then ask all members of society how they would wish to resolve the situations $E^1, E^2, \dots$ All those individuals who accept the equity axiom will, of course, say that for E^1 alternative x should be the preferred state. For a moment, let us focus on just one member of the society. Will he or she find x also preferable in situation E^2? If 'yes', will the same verdict hold in $E^3, E^4, \dots$? It is very possible that at some point in this successive questioning the individual wishes to switch from 'x preferable to y' to 'now y should be preferred to x socially'. This outcome would be in line with the Yaari and Bar-Hillel (1984) results. It could, however, also be the case that, given the size of the society, the evaluating member of society would always want x to be socially preferred to y and thus follows the equity axiom unconditionally.

The situation that we shall present and discuss now can be found on the internet together with several other cases. The structure of all situations is similar to the one in our $E^1, E^2, \ldots$ profiles above. There is always one (group of) person(s) who is worst-off under both alternatives x and y and, therefore, needier than the others. That person is better-off under x than under y whereas all the other (groups of) individuals who are introduced successively are better-off under y than under x. This situation as well as the others were presented to classes of undergraduate students at the University of Osnabrück between 1989 and 2002. All students were enrolled in economics or business administration. At the time of the investigation the students had not yet had a course on welfare economics and theories of distributive justice, such as utilitarianism, Rawlsianism and game-theoretical solutions.[7]

Here is the situation we wish to focus on.

Q 3.7:

(o) A small society has received a certain amount of money which can be used either to provide some help and assistance for a handicapped person or to further the education of an intelligent child. The child could receive a good education in languages and in natural sciences, let's say. Let the handicapped person be person 1; if the sum of money were used for her support (alternative x), she would be able to learn some very basic things, so that at least in certain areas of daily life she would no longer be totally dependent on the assistance from other people. Let the intelligent child be

---

[7] The website is http://www.vwl-theorie.uni-osnabrueck.de/darp.pdf. All in all, six different situations were given to the students. All these situations are fully reproduced in Gaertner and Jungeilges (2002). In Osnabrück, there were two versions of the questionnaire, a technical and a non-technical version (the technical version is reproduced here and on the internet). The non-technical version did not use the specification in terms of extended orderings but provided a somewhat lengthier verbal description of the same 'facts' instead. Of course, each student only saw one version. Table 3.4 (p. 47) gives the results from the non-technical version only. The Osnabrück results for the two versions did not show any difference on the basis of a two-sample non-parametric test, given an error probability of 5%.

person 2; the investment into her education represents alternative
y. The interpersonal welfare ranking reads:

$(y, 2)(x, 2)(x, 1)(y, 1)$.

Which alternative should be realized in your view, x or y?

(a) Imagine that the sum of money which could be used to help the
handicapped person is so large that, on the other hand, this
amount would suffice for the education of not only person 2 but
also a second child (person 3) who is even more intelligent
than person 2. Person 3 would, therefore, benefit even a bit more
from the education so that the following interpersonal welfare
ranking can be assumed:

$(y, 3)(y, 2)(x, 3)(x, 2)(x, 1)(y, 1)$.

Would you choose x or y under these conditions?

(b) Imagine that if the money were used to finance alternative y it
would be possible to educate still another child (person 4). The
reason may simply be 'economies of scale' or the fact that a
talented teacher will be able to provide a good education for
several children simultaneously. Let us assume that all the other
characteristics of the situation remain as before. The
interpersonal welfare ranking now reads:

$(y, 4)(y, 3)(y, 2)(x, 4)(x, 3)(x, 2)(x, 1)(y, 1)$.

Which alternative should be picked in your view, x or y?

(c) Add another child to the situation (person 5), who could also
receive an instruction in languages and the natural sciences out
of the given budget. Everything else remains the same and the
interpersonal welfare ranking reads:

$(y, 5)(y, 4)(y, 3)(y, 2)(x, 5)(x, 4)(x, 3)(x, 2)(x, 1)(y, 1)$.

Would you want x or y to be realized?

The issue is to allocate a certain amount of money to provide
some help for a handicapped person (alternative x) or to teach one

(or several) intelligent child(ren). Clearly, the intelligent child(ren) is (are) always better-off than the handicapped person whatever decision will be taken. When we compare the current situation with the various cases presented by Yaari and Bar-Hillel, we can with some justification argue that the present situation again reflects the needs aspect.[8] The students most likely played the role of an external judge. In other words, their identification with the position and the circumstances of a particular person was only of an indirect nature. On a second thought, however, this need not necessarily have been the case. Imagine that a student himself (herself) turned out to be handicapped or that one member within his (her) family or a close friend suffered from a handicap. We do not know this, of course, but had it been the case it would certainly have mattered. Moreover, there is a crucial difference between this setup and that of Yaari and Bar-Hillel. In the setup of Gaertner, the *same* respondents (students) were confronted with the different variants (o)–(c).

In Table 3.4, we give the results for the Osnabrück students during the period 1989–2002. Explaining the digits and numbers in this table, 0 always represents the choice of alternative x, 1 stands for the choice of alternative y. In order to be more explicit, the sequence 0000, for example, refers to those students who took a decision in favour of x in all cases, i.e. in the basic situation and in all of its variants. The sequences 0001, 0011 and 0111 represent the verdicts of those respondents who decided at one point to revise their original judgment. The numbers in the columns give the percentages of answers within each of the cohorts of undergraduates. Relative frequencies of a revision or 'switch' are contained in the lower part of the table. All those sequences which begin with 0 represent students who satisfied the equity axiom in the basic situation. Correspondingly, all those sequences which start with 1 hint at a violation of the equity

---

[8] Note that the situation also contains an aspect of productivity, since an investment in human capital usually leads to a general increase in efficiency, at least in the longer run.

Table 3.4. *Testing the equity axiom*

				Year of investigation				
				1989	1990	1993	1994	2002
		Sequence		$n = 65$	$n = 93$	$n = 81$	$n = 63$	$n = 86$
0	0	0	0	72.3	58.1	49.4	60.3	40.7
0	0	0	1	4.6	8.6	6.2	1.6	3.5
0	0	1	0	0.0	0.0	0.0	0.0	0.0
0	0	1	1	7.7	15.1	14.8	9.5	17.4
0	1	0	0	0.0	0.0	0.0	0.0	0.0
0	1	0	1	0.0	0.0	0.0	0.0	0.0
0	1	1	0	0.0	0.0	0.0	0.0	1.2
0	1	1	1	7.7	8.6	17.3	14.3	23.3
1	0	0	0	0.0	0.0	0.0	0.0	0.0
1	0	0	1	0.0	0.0	0.0	0.0	0.0
1	0	1	0	0.0	0.0	0.0	0.0	0.0
1	0	1	1	0.0	0.0	0.0	0.0	0.0
1	1	0	0	0.0	1.1	0.0	0.0	0.0
1	1	0	1	0.0	0.0	0.0	0.0	0.0
1	1	1	0	0.0	0.0	0.0	0.0	0.0
1	1	1	1	7.7	8.6	12.3	14.3	14.0
% of switch				19.8	32.1	38.3	25.4	44.2
% fulfilment of equity axiom				92.3	90.3	87.7	85.7	86.0

axiom. The percentages of students who satisfied the equity axiom in the two-person case are given at the bottom of the table.

Let us try to interpret the findings. We start with the year 1989. In the base year, the equity axiom was fulfilled by not less than 92.3% of the respondents. Only 7.7% of the respondents wanted the amount of money to go into the education of the intelligent child(ren) right away. Moreover, the decision to give the money to the handicapped person in all cases, i.e. unconditionally, was also very strong (72.3%).

Those who wished to revise their original decision which, at the out-set, was in favour of helping the handicapped were 19.8% of the students. The percentages of those who wanted to revise their decision after the first or second 'round' were equally high (7.7%).

When we now examine the following years, we see that the per-centages for an unconditional support of the handicapped have more or less continually gone down. At the same time, the unconditional support for an education of the talented child(ren) as well as the desire to switch already after the first round experienced a steady increase over the years (the latter from 7.7% in 1989 to 23.3% in 2002). All these developments are reflected in a steady decline of the fulfilment of the equity axiom and in a considerable increase of the desire to revise an originally made decision (from 19.8% in 1989 to 44.2% in 2002). Students were invited to give a verbal explanation of the reasons for their answers. These explanations revealed that the continual decline of unconditional sup-port for the worst-off and the simultaneous increase in support of an education of talented children can, at least to some degree, be explained by a growing attention to aspects of efficiency.

These tendencies or differences, rather, that evolved over time were checked statistically by using a χ^2 test with the H_o hypothesis of an identical distribution of the responses between any two cohorts (years). The results of these tests are such that the H_o hypothesis was rejected at the 5% significance level between the cohorts of 1989 and 1993 and between 1989 and 2002. Furthermore, the H_o hypothesis was rejected at the 10% level between the years 1994 and 2002. So the statistical analysis confirms what has become apparent from a purely descriptive comparison: the respondents to a considerable degree turned away from an unconditional support of the worse-off and devel-oped a greater concern for the better-off.

The situation depicted above was given to students in other countries. Gaertner *et al.* (2001) ran their questionnaire studies in Austria, the Baltics, Israel and Slovenia, among other countries. The Israeli results turned out to be quite close to the German figures. However, the results from the Baltic countries, as summarized in

Table 3.5. *The equity axiom: results for the Baltic states*

Sequence	The Baltics 1997–98 $n = 67$	Vilnius 2001 $n = 97$
0000	3.0	4.1
0001	0.0	1.0
0010	4.5	0.0
0011	17.9	8.2
0100	0.0	1.0
0101	1.5	0.0
0110	4.5	0.0
0111	34.3	25.8
1000	1.5	0.0
1001	1.5	0.0
1010	1.5	0.0
1011	3.0	0.0
1100	1.5	1.0
1101	1.5	2.1
1110	0.0	1.0
1111	23.9	55.7
% of switch	52.2	35.0
% of fulfilment of equity axiom	65.7	40.1

Table 3.5, were vastly different. The percentage of respondents supporting the handicapped person unconditionally (and therefore opting for the sequence 0000) was less than 5%. Austria and Slovenia were somewhere 'in between'.

The finding of differences in responses over time and between countries raises interesting theoretical issues. Is it possible or desirable to formulate a universal theory of justice if the responses of individuals are not stable over time and appear to be influenced crucially by their social, political and historical context? We will return to this question in the concluding Chapter 6. For the moment, we can safely say that the support for the difference principle is not unconditional in that for most respondents from a certain point onwards efficiency considerations start to play a significant role.

3.3 FROM BEING AN OUTSIDE OBSERVER TO BEING INVOLVED UNDER A VEIL

An additional perspective on the debate between utilitarianism and maximin is offered by the theoretical concept of the 'original position', in which individuals evaluate social institutions behind a 'veil of ignorance', i.e. in the hypothetical situation that they do not know their own relative position in society. Harsanyi argued that economic decisions taken in such a hypothetical situation would be free of any personal bias:

> a value judgment on the distribution of income would show the required impersonality to the highest degree if the person who made this judgment had to choose a particular income distribution in complete ignorance of what his own relative position ... would be within the system chosen. This would be the case if he had exactly the same chance of obtaining the first position (corresponding to the highest income) or the second or the third, etc. up to the last position (corresponding to the lowest income) available within that scheme.
>
> (Harsanyi, 1953, pp. 434–5)

Moreover, Harsanyi stated that a rational decision-maker in this hypothetical situation would opt for a utilitarian decision rule. Remarkably, Rawls (1971) introduced a similar idea of the original position, but the conclusions he drew from it were very different. Notice that the Rawlsian veil is much thicker than the one proposed by Harsanyi. For Rawls, it is not only the case that no one knows their place in society, their position or social status, Rawls also assumes that the parties do not know the particular circumstances of their own society. In other words, they do not know its economic and political situation, or the level of civilization and culture it has been able to achieve (Rawls, 1971, §24). Rawls rejected Harsanyi's decision-theoretic approach in terms of probabilities and claimed that individuals in the original position would opt for the difference principle. In fact, as we will see, Harsanyi himself has also proposed two different approaches to support utilitarianism.

This debate raises deep methodological issues. Is the veil of ignorance an attractive approach for thinking about justice? Are risky decisions in the original position able to capture ethical judgments on distributive justice? If 'yes', would decision-makers in the original position support utilitarianism or rather maximin? Some questionnaire studies have explored these questions. Moreover, in this setting there are also some interesting laboratory experiments. We will discuss the latter in section 3.4.

The study that comes closest to the basic inspiration of Harsanyi has been set up by Amiel *et al.* (2009). In their questionnaire experiments, the focus is on Harsanyi's two utilitarian models. In both models the objective of social choice consists in ranking all possible (uncertain) social outcomes *p*, where the social outcome *p* can be seen as a vector of the (uncertain) outcomes for all the *n* individuals in society. In the first of Harsanyi's two models – commonly referred to as 'Harsanyi's aggregation theorem' (Weymark, 1991) – it is assumed that the preferences of all individuals and the social preference relation over the social outcomes *p* satisfy the expected utility axioms. If one imposes in addition the criterion of Pareto Indifference (if all individuals are indifferent between two outcomes *p* and *p'*, the social planner is also indifferent between *p* and *p'*), then Harsanyi claims that one can write

$$V(p) = \sum_{i=1}^{n} a_i V_i(p) + b$$

where $V(p)$ measures the social utility of outcome *p* and $V_i(p)$ the individual utility of individual *i* in *p*.[9]

---

[9] Stated more formally: if V_i and V are the von Neumann–Morgenstern utility representations of the individual preference relations and the social preference relation, respectively then, given that Pareto Indifference is satisfied, there exist numbers

The aggregation theorem derives social utility as the weighted sum of individual utilities. However, it does not say that the weights a_i have to be positive or at least non-negative. Nor does it say that the vector of coefficients $(a_1, \ldots, a_n; b)$ is unique. Furthermore, this mathematical representation theorem does not assume the possibility of interpersonal utility comparisons. Harsanyi (1978, p. 227) says that if such comparisons are ruled out, then the coefficients a_i will have to be based completely on the evaluating person's 'personal – and more or less arbitrary – value judgments'.[10] In this first approach, the evaluator is *not* necessarily a member of the society that he is examining. Harsanyi (1978, p. 226) mentions judges and other public officials who will be 'guided in their official capacities by some notions of public interest and of impartial justice'. However, as we have seen, the evaluating person's moral preferences have to satisfy certain Bayesian rationality postulates (implying expected utility) so that 'his moral value judgments will be such as if he tried to maximize a special utility function expressing these moral preferences' (1978, p. 226). This utility function will be the evaluator's social welfare function.

The second model – often referred to as the 'impartial observer theorem' – is based on the intuition of the 'veil of ignorance' and was discussed by Harsanyi in a number of contributions (Harsanyi 1953, 1955, 1977, 1978). The basic idea is already to be found in Vickrey (1945). This model presupposes the possibility of interpersonal comparisons of utility. This is done in the way that an impartial observer[11]

$a_i, i \in \{1, \ldots, n\}$, and b such that for all elements p from a set of lotteries L, $V(p)$ is a weighted affine combination of the individual utilities $V_i(p)$.

[10] The vector of coefficients $(a_1, \ldots, a_n)$ can be rendered strictly positive by replacing Pareto Indifference by Strong Pareto (i.e. if social outcome p is strictly better than p' for at least one individual, while no individual strictly prefers p' to p, then the social planner prefers p to p'). The vector of coefficients $(a_1, \ldots, a_n; b)$ becomes unique by introducing a further requirement that Harsanyi did not make explicitly. This is the axiom of Independent Prospects, which says that for each individual one can find a pair of prospects over which that person is not indifferent and over which every other individual is indifferent.

[11] The term 'impartial observer' may be considered a somewhat confusing misnomer, particularly in relation to Adam Smith's notion of an 'impartial spectator', put forward in 'The Theory of Moral Sentiments' (1759). In this work, Smith argues that the requirement of impartiality demands the invoking of disinterested

who is sympathetic to the interests of each member of society makes moral value judgments for this society. More explicitly, the observer is to imagine himself being person i, $i \in \{1, \ldots, n\}$, under social alternatives x, y, etc. In making this sympathetic identification with individual i, the observer not only considers himself with i's objective circumstances under $x, y, \ldots$, but also is supposed to imagine himself with i's subjective characteristics, in particular with i's preference ordering. In order to be impartial, the observer has to enter a thought experiment in which he is imagining that he has an equal chance of being any person in society, complete with that person's objective and subjective circumstances. In this way, an equal consideration is given to each person's interests. In ranking the social outcomes p, the impartial observer, person j – but it can be any $j \in \{1, \ldots, n\}$ – calculates the average expected utility over all individuals, so that one arrives at the formula of the arithmetic mean:

$$W_j(p) = \frac{1}{n} \sum_{i=1}^{n} V_i(p).$$

The expression on the right-hand side of this formula is person j's expected utility.

Several authors have drawn attention to conceptual difficulties with Harsanyi's two models (see, e.g., Mongin, 2001 and Weymark, 1991). However, Harsanyi distinguished between them and took some care to point out, as mentioned above, that the first model does not presuppose that individual utilities be comparable across persons whereas the second model would be meaningless without such a requirement.

In their questionnaire experiment, Amiel et al. (2009) focus on one of the crucial differences between both models, i.e. the role and position of the person who makes an evaluation for society. They ask their respondents to express their views on two income distribution vectors, embedded in the context of either the first or the second model. The situations presented are based on Amiel and Cowell

judgments of any fair and impartial spectator, not necessarily belonging to the group to be evaluated.

(1998, 1999) and were originally used in a larger investigation concerning inequality and risk evaluations. For the current purpose, they were slightly rephrased in order to be as close as possible to Harsanyi, who considers welfare evaluations in terms of utilitarian ethics. The background for the questionnaires is a country (Alfaland) that consists of five different regions. These regions are identical with respect to all aspects except for the incomes of their inhabitants. Within each region, there are no income differences among the inhabitants. It is assumed that two economic policies A and B are under consideration and that one of these is to be implemented next year. It is known that the only effect of either policy will be on the income in each region. However, this effect will depend on the economic situation then prevailing in Alfaland: it is supposed that there are six different states in which Alfaland may find itself in the coming year.

Q 3.8 (pp. 55–6) shows the income distribution vectors under policies A and B for the six different situations in which Alfaland may find itself. In each situation policies A and B differ in the same way: a switch from policy A to policy B would represent a simple notional income transfer from a richer to a poorer region. The notional transfer affects different regions as one goes from situation 1 to situation 6. Applying the Pigou–Dalton transfer principle (one of the cornerstones of traditional inequality measurement) would imply that inequality is lower under policy B than under policy A in all situations.

There are two versions of the question. In the first, respondents are asked to put themselves in the shoes of an *outside observer* who has to evaluate policies A and B. In the second, they are asked to imagine that *they themselves* are assigned to one of the regions of Alfaland, with equal probability of finding themselves in one of the five regions. Version H1 thus stands for the Harsanyi model with an outside observer, H2 represents the model where the observer himself is a member of the society to be evaluated, with probability $1/n$ for each of the possible positions. In both versions, the respondents were asked to state which policy would, in their own opinion, lead to a *better* situation. This implies that they had to form their own ideas of what a 'better' situation for Alfaland would mean. Note that asking what is the better situation is different from asking what is the most unequal situation. In Harsanyi's models a positive or negative net effect on overall utilitarian welfare would depend on the properties of the individual utility functions. In his second model, with a common weight of $1/n$ attached to the utility functions of all n agents, a case of 'relatively similar' strictly concave utility functions for all persons in society would, 'with high probability', lead to the assertion that aggregate welfare is higher under policy B than under policy A.

Q 3.8 (H1): Alfaland consists of five regions that are identical in every respect other than the incomes of their inhabitants. Everyone within a given region receives the same income, but personal incomes differ from region to region.

Two economic policy proposals A and B are being considered for implementation in Alfaland next year. It is known that – apart from their impact on personal incomes – the two policies would have the same effect on the population. The impact upon the regions' incomes would depend upon the particular state of the Alfaland economy at the time the policy (A or B) is to be introduced.

In each of questions (1) to (6) two alternative lists of incomes A and B (in Alfaland local currency) are given. Each of these pairs represents the outcomes of the A policy and the B policy on the five regions in each of six different situations in which Alfaland might find itself next year. Imagine that you are invited to be an outside observer of Alfaland. In each case please state which policy you consider would result in a better situation in Alfaland by circling A or B. If you consider that the two policies will result in an equivalent situation then circle both A and B:

(1) $A = (2, 5, 9, 20, 30)$ $B = (2, 6, 8, 20, 30)$

(2) $A = (2, 5, 9, 20, 30)$ $B = (3, 5, 9, 20, 29)$

(3) $A = (2, 5, 9, 20, 30)$ $B = (2, 6, 9, 20, 29)$

(4) $A = (2, 5, 9, 20, 30)$ $B = (2, 10, 9, 15, 30)$

(5) $A = (10\ 10, 10, 10, 30)$		$B = (10, 10, 10, 20, 20)$
(6) $A = (2, 5, 9, 20, 30)$		$B = (2, 6, 9, 19, 30)$

Q 3.9 (H2): The same as Q 3.8 except for the third sentence in the third paragraph, that is replaced by:

Imagine that you have been assigned to one of the regions in Alfaland with an equal chance of being in any one of the five regions.

The questions were presented to samples of student respondents in a series of experimental sessions during 2003. All were first-year or second-year students of economics or business administration and came from the UK (LSE), Germany (Osnabrück) and Israel (Ruppin). In each case the respondents completed the exercise during class or lecture time and were randomly assigned an H1-type or H2-type questionnaire.

We start with the overall results from all three countries. In Table 3.6 the six possible situations for Alfaland are labelled Q_1 to Q_6. For each individual situation, we state the percentage of answers that find that policy B leads to a better situation in Alfaland than policy A, for all respondents and for males and for females separately. Although from previous studies there is evidence of rejection of the principle of transfers in the context of both inequality and of social welfare (Amiel and Cowell, 1999), it was not clear *a priori* what response should be expected when comparing the two variants of the Harsanyi model. However, it is clear from the combined sample (Table 3.6) that there is a well-defined pattern: the proportions of B responses in the outside-observer model vector dominate those in the model with involvement. The pattern is slightly less clear-cut when broken down by males and females.[12]

---

[12] A small-sample paired t test for differences shows that the proportion of B responses is significantly higher (at the 1% level) in H1 compared with H2. Considering males alone, there is a dominance of H1 over H2 (significant at the 5% level) in five of the six questions; clearly question 4 is the exception. For the female subsample the proportion of B responses is higher in H1 for only four out of six questions, and the results are not significant.

Table 3.6. *Harsanyi's models: responses from all countries*

	N	Q_1	Q_2	Q_3	Q_4	Q_5	Q_6
				% choosing policy B			
				Males			
H1	76	63.2	81.6	72.4	61.8	85.5	61.8
H2	82	51.2	74.4	70.7	64.6	81.7	56.1
				Females			
H1	62	54.8	79.0	72.6	59.7	74.2	51.6
H2	64	60.9	84.4	59.4	45.3	70.3	50.0
				All			
H1	138	58.9	80.9	72.3	61.0	80.9	56.0
H2	146	55.0	78.5	65.8	57.0	76.5	53.7

It is instructive to check whether there are systematic differences between the groups of respondents in each of the locations where the experiment was conducted. The results for the country subsamples are summarized in Tables 3.7–3.9. For the UK subsample, there is again vector dominance of H1 responses over H2 responses (last two rows of Table 3.7). This vector dominance, which also holds for the female students, does not hold for males.[13] For Germany, the results are similar (Table 3.8). For the whole sample, there is vector dominance of H1 over H2 (at the 2% significance level). This time, the male percentages show a vector dominance of H1 over H2 (also at the 2% level); for the female responses, nothing like this happens. All in all, the evidence for the UK and Germany suggests that there is a greater propensity to conform to standard norms of distributional

---

[13] The paired t test for differences is highly significant for males and females combined (significance level below 1%). For females alone H1 dominates at a 5% significance level. For males the proportion of B responses for H1 is greater than or equal to those for H2 in all but one case but the differences are not significant.

Table 3.7. *Responses from UK subsample*

| | N | % choosing policy B | | | | | |
		Q_1	Q_2	Q_3	Q_4	Q_5	Q_6
				Males			
H1	24	62.5	79.2	70.8	66.7	79.2	62.5
H2	30	56.7	66.7	73.3	66.7	73.3	60.0
				Females			
H1	18	72.2	88.9	83.3	83.3	83.3	72.2
H2	13	53.8	69.2	46.2	38.5	46.2	38.5
				All			
H1	42	65.1	83.7	76.7	74.4	81.4	65.1
H2	43	54.5	68.2	65.9	59.1	65.9	54.5

Table 3.8. *Responses from German subsample*

| | N | % choosing policy B | | | | | |
		Q_1	Q_2	Q_3	Q_4	Q_5	Q_6
				Males			
H1	31	74.2	80.6	80.6	64.5	93.5	74.2
H2	28	46.4	67.9	57.1	53.6	85.7	39.3
				Females			
H1	17	47.1	70.6	70.6	58.8	76.5	35.3
H2	24	62.5	79.2	45.8	37.5	75.0	50.0
				All			
H1	48	64.6	77.1	77.1	62.5	87.5	60.4
H2	52	53.8	73.1	51.9	46.2	80.8	44.2

Table 3.9. *Responses from Israeli subsample*

	N	Q_1	Q_2	Q_3	Q_4	Q_5	Q_6
				% choosing policy B			
				Males			
H1	21	47.6	85.7	61.9	52.4	81.0	42.9
H2	24	50.0	91.7	83.3	75.0	87.5	70.8
				Females			
H1	27	48.1	77.8	66.7	44.4	66.7	48.1
H2	27	63.0	96.3	77.8	55.6	77.8	55.6
				All			
H1	48	48.0	82.0	64.0	48.0	74.0	44.0
H2	52	56.6	92.5	79.2	66.0	81.1	62.3

rankings, i.e. to accept the Pigou–Dalton transfer principle, if the issue is posed in terms of the Harsanyi outside-observer model rather than in terms of involvement.

One should be cautious in drawing too strong conclusions, however. In contrast to the evidence of dominance of H1 over H2 for both the UK and Germany subsamples, for the Israel subsample significant differences in response patterns are found *in the opposite direction* – see Table 3.9. There is vector dominance with respect to H2 in all three cases, i.e. the complete sample and the two breakdowns for males and females.[14] The reasons for the difference between the Israel subsample and the rest might be supposed to lie in demographic or other background factors. Some information about such factors was collected for all three countries, e.g. whether respondents were employed before entering university, what their income expectations were and where

---

[14] Significant at the 1% level for males and females combined, and at the 5% level for males or females taken separately.

they would locate their political views (on a left to right axis). All these characteristics did not prove to be statistically significant for explaining the response patterns. Moreover, rerunning the Israel questionnaire experiment in 2005 with a new sample of students fully confirmed the earlier results from 2003, apart from some minor differences in the gender breakdown.

A person who asserts that policy B leads to a better situation for Alfaland than policy A must be convinced that an income transfer from a richer region to a poorer region is welfare-increasing for the country. The supposition for this is, of course, that the person has the all-encompassing concept of welfare in mind that economists normally use. If the utility functions of the representative in each of the five regions are identical and strictly concave, the welfare-improving effect is unambiguous and independent of where the transfer occurs. But this conclusion does not necessarily hold if the curvature of the utility function is different for persons in different regions: marginal utility losses have to be compared with marginal utility gains and the net effect can be of any sign.

How to explain, then, the apparent differences between the country subsamples in the responses to the outside-observer model and the model where the evaluating person is involved? One might be tempted to label these as just 'cultural differences' but they may also be understood in terms of different attitudes to risk. The risk argument for the difference in response patterns would run as follows. Personal attitude towards risk is absent under model H1 but is central to H2 (remember that Harsanyi himself characterized the case of an impartial but involved observer as a clear instance of a choice involving risk). So, consider the position characterizing the UK and Germany respondents: from an outside point of view (where self-interest is not an issue and personal risks are not involved) they find the argument that a richer-to-poorer transfer is welfare-increasing more convincing than if they were personally affected. By contrast, in a risky situation, Israeli respondents appreciate a richer-to-poorer transfer more when they are involved than they do from the position of an outside observer. It is also possible that the respondents in all three countries clearly view H2 as a situation involving risk, whereas they look upon H1 as a case to which a utilitarian calculus should not be applied. The sharp difference between Germany and the UK, on the one hand, and Israel, on the other, would then come from the different ways in which these two groups view H1. This would definitely imply that the attitude of an outside observer is different from the position taken from behind a veil of ignorance.

Having spoken about the aspect of risk, we would like to briefly report some results from a companion paper by Amiel *et al.* (2008). In this investigation the risk phenomenon was *explicitly* introduced into the evaluation of income vectors in Alfaland. This was done by replacing the fourth sentence in the third paragraph of the description of Q 3.8 starting with 'In each case please state which policy you consider ...' with the following two variants that we denote as 'risk' and 'risk-involved', respectively: (a) 'In each case please state which policy you consider would result in higher risk for a person immigrating to Alfaland by circling A or B'; (b) 'In each case please state which policy you consider would result in higher risk for you as an immigrant to Alfaland by circling A or B'.[15] The reason for these two versions was to see whether in a situation focusing on the risk aspect, one would obtain different results for the outside-observer case as compared to the situation of being personally involved, similar to the two Harsanyi variants discussed above. This was indeed the case, as Table 3.10 shows. The respondents of the two variants of risk and risk-involved come from the same series of experimental sessions during 2003 from which the Harsanyi results were taken. The students who evaluated the risk scenarios were, of course, different from those who responded to the two Harsanyi versions.

The percentage of respondents choosing policy A is in five of the six situations higher in the outside-observer case than in the involvement case. If we lump together the figures from the risk investigation

---

[15] Notice that what in Amiel *et al.* (2008) was called the 'orthodox position' would require answer A in this case of risk while it would require answer B in the two Harsanyi versions.

Table 3.10. *Risk: responses from all countries*

	N	Q$_1$	Q$_2$	Q$_3$	Q$_4$	Q$_5$	Q$_6$
				% choosing policy A			
Risk	140	41.4	57.9	57.1	56.4	57.9	48.6
Risk-inv.	142	41.5	54.9	50.7	47.2	56.3	42.3

Table 3.11. *Involvement versus non-involvement*

	N	Q$_1$	Q$_2$	Q$_3$	Q$_4$	Q$_5$	Q$_6$
				% choosing the orthodox position			
Non-involved	278	50.2	69.4	64.8	58.7	69.4	52.3
Involved	288	48.5	67.0	58.4	52.2	66.7	48.1

and from the Harsanyi investigation, i.e. if we lump together figures expressing the orthodox view (see n. 15) and denote the overall figures by 'non-involved' and 'involved', we obtain the results shown in Table 3.11.

As can be easily seen, there is vector dominance of the elements in the first row over those in the second row. While the figures in Table 3.10 are, qualitatively speaking, in conformity with the overall results in the lower part of Table 3.6, the aggregated figures in Table 3.11 again highlight one of the major issues in this section: the position from where situations are being evaluated seems to be of considerable importance.

It may be of interest for the reader to compare further the results in Table 3.10 with the figures in the bottom part of Table 3.6. For all six questions the frequency of taking the orthodox position is significantly lower in the risk variants than it is in the two Harsanyi versions, both for the non-involved and the involved case. When one compares the wording in the risk cases with the one in H1 and H2, one might argue that, in the former, the wording has a negative connotation ('would result in higher risk'), whereas under Harsanyi, the connotation is positive ('would result in a better situation'). This could be a reason for the large differences between the two tables. It may also be the case that a situation involving risk is more complicated to evaluate than a situation where an improvement in terms of overall welfare is the issue. It is very possible that both explanations (and several more) come into play simultaneously (for more details, see Amiel *et al.*, 2008).

Two other questionnaire studies throw additional light on this issue. Although these studies are less strongly rooted in the social choice literature than the investigation by Amiel *et al.* (2009), some of their results are revealing. Bernasconi (2002) and Bosmans and Schokkaert (2004) draw a distinction between three different positions. Bosmans and Schokkaert call these the 'impartial and sympathetic observer' (ISO), the 'rational individual behind the veil of ignorance' (VOI) and 'purely individual risk preferences' (PIR), respectively. The first two coincide with models H1 and H2 in Amiel *et al.* (2009), the latter is a refinement. The basic idea is that VOI preferences are preferences over lotteries that have complete income distributions as outcomes, while PIR preferences are over lotteries with individual incomes as outcomes. Differences between VOI and PIR preferences can result from the fact that individuals do not care only about their own incomes but also, for instance, about overall equality or about their own relative income position. To illustrate the distinctions it is useful to look at the specific formulations that have been used in the questionnaire of Bosmans and Schokkaert (2004). They confronted different groups of Belgian undergraduate business students with three versions of a related problem. In each of the versions eight different questions were asked. For illustrative purposes, we show only one of these eight questions:[16]

---

[16] For the ISO version, the VOI version and the PIR version, there were, respectively, 93, 92 and 94 respondents.

Q 3.10 (ISO): Consider the situation of two firms, A and B, that each plan to employ 100 recently graduated students. Assume that in each firm there are three types of jobs that are identical in all respects but yield a different monthly net income. The first job yields €2,500, the second €1,500 and the third €500. The firms differ however with respect to the numbers of positions they have available for each of the three jobs. Evidently, due to the different distributions of incomes, the global welfare of the 100 employees can be different in firms A and B. We are interested in your personal judgments of these welfare differences. Indicate in each of the eight questions below which firm leads to the highest welfare according to you:

	A	B
Question 3	25 earn €1,500 each, 75 earn €500 each	20 earn €2,500 each, 80 earn €500 each

Q 3.11 (VOI): Try to put yourself in the position of a recently graduated student who has to choose, just as 99 other recently graduated students, between accepting a job in firm A or in firm B. Assume that in each firm there are three types of jobs that are identical in all respects but yield a different monthly net income. The first job yields €2,500, the second €1,500 and the third €500. The firms differ however with respect to the numbers of positions they have available for each of the three jobs. You and the 99 other recently graduated students either all end up in firm A or all in firm B. Each of the 100 of you has an equal probability of ending up in each of the 100 positions. So, it is unknown beforehand which job you will get. Indicate in each of the eight questions below which firm you would prefer.

Q 3.12 (PIR): Try to put yourself in the position of a recently graduated student who has to choose between accepting a job in firm A or in firm B. Assume that in each firm there are three types of jobs that are identical in all respects but yield a different monthly net income. The first job yields €2,500, the second €1,500 and the third €500. The firms differ however with respect to the numbers of positions they have available for each of the three jobs. Beforehand it is not known with certainty which of the three possible jobs you will eventually get. Your chances are different in both firms. Indicate in each of the eight questions below which firm you would prefer.

A related but different formulation is used by Bernasconi (2002). Both Bernasconi (2002) and Bosmans and Schokkaert (2004) find that the expected utility approach is far from being generally accepted in their samples of students. In the study of Bosmans and Schokkaert (2004), the proportion of respondents that satisfy the axioms of expected utility theory, taking the eight questions for each version together, is between 10% and 13% for all three versions. This result is in line with the common finding that respondents in an experimental setting do not maximize expected utility. Note, however, that acceptance of the expected utility criterion in the VOI case is the basic justification of utilitarianism by Harsanyi. Bosmans and Schokkaert then look more carefully at the direction in which their respondents depart from expected utility. Testing for the homogeneity of the answers on similar questions in the three versions, their most important finding is that the response patterns are different for the three versions, with VOI preferences in between ISO and PIR preferences.[17] This is exactly what one would expect *a priori*: ISO preferences deal exclusively with uninvolved common interest, PIR preferences deal exclusively with involved self-interest and VOI preferences deal with involved self-interest and VOI preferences deal with involved common interest (that is, the common interest is at stake). The difference between ISO and VOI confirms the finding of Amiel *et al.* (2009) that the preferences of an outside impartial observer are not the same as the preferences of an involved individual behind the veil of ignorance. The

---

[17] At a significance level of 0.05, the answers for similar questions are different between the ISO and VOI versions in two out of the eight cases, between VOI and PIR in only one case and between ISO and PIR in four out of the eight cases.

difference between VOI and PIR suggests that externalities and relative income positions may play a role in the evaluation behind the veil of ignorance. The latter point is further analysed by Carlsson *et al.* (2005) and Johansson-Stenman *et al.* (2002). They let respondents choose between different hypothetical societies for their grandchildren. The results clearly suggest that it is useful to distinguish between risk aversion and inequality aversion, with respondents showing a strong concern for relative income.

Apparently the relationship between risk preferences and ethical preferences is not straightforward, and difficult questions remain. Yet, it is fair to conclude that the results from the empirical work suggest that the preferences of a rational individual behind a veil of ignorance do not necessarily coincide with the judgments of an impartial outside observer. While the pattern of differences definitely requires further investigation, it remains striking that all the questionnaire studies described do find significant differences between the answers in both positions. This gives some support to the philosophical critics of the veil of ignorance (see, e.g., Roemer, 2002 and Sen, 2009).

The last remark takes us back to a question that we posed very early on in this section (p. 51): 'Is the veil of ignorance an attractive approach to think about justice?' Sen (2009), who compares the Smithian concept of impartial spectator with the Rawlsian construct of an original position under a veil of ignorance (Harsanyi is only indirectly discussed – see footnote on p. 198 in Sen, 2009), strongly supports Smith's position of open impartiality that he contrasts with 'the "closed" nature of the participatory exercise that Rawls invokes through restricting the "veil of ignorance" to the members of a given focal group' (Sen, 2009, p. 133). Sen goes so far as to call Rawls' confinement to those who are immediately involved a form of parochialism while Smith's idea induces a 'broadening of admissible voices beyond the confines of the local territory or polity' (Sen, 2009, p. 135). A broadening of views, incorporating as much valuable information as possible, also led Konow, in some recent work, to the assertion that the veil of ignorance cannot be an attractive approach to reflect upon justice. Konow (2009b) develops the idea of a 'quasi–spectator' – 'this is an observer who has no salient stakes in the matter at hand and possesses some, if not all, information relevant to his internalized moral values' (2009b, p. 106). Konow seeks a kind of impartiality that is associated with a high level of information and results in consensus. According to the author (Konow, 2009a), the impartial spectator has three fundamental characteristics: impartiality, information and sympathy. The impartial observer is a disinterested third party, not guided by any trace of self-interest. Furthermore, this person who is not real but imagined is fully informed of the relevant particulars of a situation to be assessed and, lastly, the spectator exercises sympathy towards the others which enables him to understand their experiences and share their feelings. This construct of an impartial spectator, we believe, comes close to Harsanyi's first model that we discussed at the beginning of this section, though, in the present context, without any trace of Bayesian rationality. Konow (2009b) asserts that the ideal of the impartial spectator can be recognized in many real social institutions; examples are judges, juries and independent arbitrators who are supposed to be third parties 'who seek all relevant information on the issues they are deciding' (2009b, p. 106).

Since perfect impartiality can never be achieved, one can at best observe the judgments of a quasi-spectator, Konow argues. The author's study focuses on consensus as a test of spectator impartiality. 'The prediction is that increasing relevant information will, on average, increase convergence (i.e. reduce dispersion) of the moral views of quasi-spectators' (2009b, p. 107). This is, of course, in sharp contrast to those who propagate a thick veil of ignorance as the basis for unanimous or at least convergent moral judgments. Remember Rawls' verdict of unanimous agreement behind a veil of ignorance. Therefore, the null hypothesis that is tested in the author's statistical analysis is that information has no effect on convergence of judgments. In the eight vignettes or hypothetical scenarios that the author gave to a wide range of students at Loyola Marymount University during the years 2003–6, a distinction was made between a high- and a low-information mode. Consensus consistent with the quasi-spectator model is then seen as a reduction in the variance around the respective means in the high-information versus the low-information treatments. The overall results over the eight vignettes that stretch from aspects of efficiency and need to issues in bioethics and business ethics indeed show that increased relevant information will, on average, reduce variance: 'Variance falls with increased relevant information due to the improved capacity of agents to reason from a common set of values' (2009b, p. 117).

Denying that more and more precise information will lead to better judgments would be very strange indeed. And to find that people's judgments will converge, if this information is generally considered as valid and reliable, should not come as a surprise either. Konow writes that 'one must observe the marginal effect of information, i.e., information must be varied *incrementally*' (2009b, p. 108, our italics). And it is precisely here that we have some doubts. In some of the vignettes, the high-information modes contain the only piece of precise information while the low-information modes leave the external observer in a cloud of mist. We therefore doubt that the difference between high and low information can be viewed as 'marginal' or 'incremental'. One could perhaps even ask to what degree the (or some of the) high-information modes are to some extent manipulative, *by necessity* yielding the results that the author achieved. Let us clarify our point a bit more by reproducing vignettes 2 and 3 which focus on needs and accountability, respectively.

> **Q 3.13 (low-information)**: The state provides support to those in need for a limited period of time. For example, John, who needs 1 year to complete a high school diploma, is eligible to receive such support. How much do you think the state should provide in total support for John per month (Enter a number from $0 to $1,000)?
>
> **Q 3.13 (high-information)**: Same text but insert after the second sentence: 'The state has determined that the basic needs of a person living in this area for food, housing and clothing equal $800 per month.'

The results are:

– for the low-information mode: 444 (mean); 68,736 (variance)
– for the high-information mode: 771 (mean); 43,759 (variance)

> **Q 3.14 (low-information)**: Suppose Adam and Bill worked last
> weekend stuffing envelopes for a mass mailing. This job took a total
> of 11 hours, but Adam worked more hours than Bill. The total pay for
> this 11-hour job is $100. How much of this $100 do you think Adam
> and Bill should each receive (Enter amounts for each person and
> make sure the two amounts total $100)?
>
> **Q 3.14 (high-information)**: Same text but insert after the second
> sentence: 'Specifically, Adam worked 8 hours, whereas Bill worked
> 3 hours.'

The results for Adam are:

– for the low-information mode: 60.2 (mean); 44.9 (variance)
– for the high-information mode: 73.4 (mean); 36.8 (variance)

We feel that in the low-information mode of both situations, the
outside observer is completely left in the dark. So in Q 3.13, an
allocation of $500 to John reveals a high degree of uneasiness on the
part of the evaluator. Then information is provided that 'the state ...
determined', and we see that the decisions of the students are close to
this number. We believe that a similar argument applies to situation
Q 3.14. The final decision to give 73.4 to Adam is very close to 8/11.
So, again, the facts given at the second stage are by no means incremental. And the observation that the variance of evaluative judgments decreases when information is given that is considered as
reliable is perhaps not very surprising.

What remains as an open question at the end of this long section
is not whether impartiality on the part of the observer can be strength-
ened by providing valuable information to the evaluating person. We
think that almost everyone will agree that adding information will

enrich the basis for judgment, though we feel, as argued above, that Konow's experimental setup was not the appropriate one to substantiate this claim. The deeper question really is whether the model of an impartial outside observer *à la* Smith or the model of an involved person under the veil of ignorance *à la* Rawls or Harsanyi is better suited for judgments on justice and injustice.

3.4 UTILITARIANISM WITH A FLOOR?

We have explained in Chapter 2 why we restrict ourselves in this book to questionnaire studies, but we also announced that we would make an exception for those experimental studies that focus on decision-making behind a veil of ignorance. The reason is obvious: the basic hypothesis of the 'veil of ignorance' approach is that rational and self-interested decision-makers behind the veil take impartial decisions that are ethically respectable. If one accepts this hypothesis, the 'veil of ignorance' approach describes a specific experimental setting that makes it possible to derive conclusions about distributive justice. We will see in subsection 3.4.1 that the experimental results are mixed. There is one striking finding, however. While in the philosophical literature (and in this chapter until now), two principles of justice are particularly prominent, namely the Rawlsian principle of focusing on the worst-off position in society and the utilitarian principle of maximizing the sum of individual utilities or maximizing the average utility in society, the experimental results suggest an additional rule. This is called the Boulding model by Traub *et al.* (2005), and boils down to utilitarianism with a floor constraint. After an overview of some experimental results, we will see in subsection 3.4.2 how this concept of utilitarianism with a floor fares in questionnaire studies.

3.4.1 Experimental results

In their seminal work, Frohlich *et al.* (1987, p. 610) started from the provocative question: 'Was Rawls right? Logically, is the floor the only concern?' They believed 'that individual analyses of choices are richer than a narrow-minded focus on the worst outcome' (1987, p. 610). They conjectured that individuals would look for a compound principle which would allow them to weigh a concern for the well-being of the poorest against an efficiency argument implicit in the principle of maximizing the average, i.e. for some rule in between maximin and utilitarianism.

The authors ran experiments at three universities in the US and Canada where students had to choose among (1) the Rawlsian principle of maximizing the floor (R), (2) the principle of maximizing the average (U), (3) the principle of maximizing the average with a floor constraint (FC) and (4) the principle of maximizing the average with a range constraint (RC). The 220 subjects were grouped five by five. First, each group was introduced to the different principles. Second, they were given a chance to discuss and then collectively choose a particular distributive principle. If the group reached consensus, payments were made according to the principle they agreed upon. If they failed to achieve consensus, they were paid according to an income distribution that was randomly chosen from the full set of possibilities.

Consensus was achieved in all groups. The groups' choices were such that out of 44 groups, 35 chose maximizing the average with a floor constraint, 7 groups reached consensus on maximizing the average and 2 groups picked the maxim of maximizing the average with a range constraint. In other words, no group ever selected maximizing the floor as their preferred principle. The Rawlsian argument that individuals in the original position would unanimously choose the maximin principle was nowhere verified. Frohlich *et al.* (1987) also asked their individual participants to rank the four principles at various stages of their experiment. Table 3.12 shows the answers to this question at the end of the experiment. Out of a total of 219 first-place ranks, maximizing the average with a floor constraint received 150 ranks while maximizing the floor only received 9. The latter principle obtained the highest number of last-place ranks (106), while the former only received 3.

Table 3.12. *Individuals' rankings of principles at the end of the experiment (Frohlich et al., 1987)*

Rankings	Maximizing the floor (R)	Maximizing the average (U)	Maximizing the average with a floor constraint (FC)	Maximizing the average with a range constraint (RC)
1st place	9	48	150	12
2nd place	30	91	52	46
3rd place	74	47	14	84
4th place	106	33	3	77

The results above are grist to the mill of those who have always argued against the Rawlsian maximin principle. However, utilitarians cannot be too happy with the findings, either. Is the overwhelming preference for maximizing the average with a floor constraint replicated in later studies? Herne and Suojanen (2004) ran a similar experiment at the University of Turku in Finland in 2002. There were 208 participants, 57% of them female. The experiment was run in groups of five students; there were 42 groups (two groups consisted of only four participants). All participants answered one choice task, called 'choice set' by the authors. Each group of five students was allocated randomly to one of three versions with slightly varying incomes (see Table 3.13). Each choice set consisted of the four alternatives that were also used by Frohlich *et al.* (1987): a utilitarian distribution (U) that maximized the average and total income, a Rawlsian distribution (R) that maximized the lowest income, a mixed distribution that maximized the average with a range constraint (RC) and a mixed distribution that maximized the average with a floor constraint (FC). The order of the alternative income distributions within each choice set was varied across the groups. The students were told that the numbers in the distributions could be understood as different net wages for 1 hour's work.

Table 3.13. *Choice sets (euros) in the Herne–Suojanen experiment*

Income class	Choice set 1				Choice set 2				Choice set 3			
	U	R	RC	FC	U	R	RC	FC	U	R	RC	FC
1	38	22	32	37	40	25	34	37	42	22	32	37
2	33	20	28	26	35	24	23	24	37	21	24	24
3	22	18	20	16	21	23	22	23	20	20	23	19
4	11	16	12	12	12	18	19	15	14	17	19	16
5	7	13	8	10	6	14	10	11	8	16	10	11
Average	22.2	17.8	20.0	20.2	22.8	20.8	21.6	22.0	24.2	19.2	21.6	21.4
Floor income	7	13	8	10	6	14	10	11	8	16	10	11
Range	31	9	24	27	34	11	24	26	34	6	22	26

Until here the setup follows Frohlich *et al.* (1987) very closely. The most interesting extension introduced by Herne and Suojanen is that they distinguish between two different experimental treatments, one in which respondents have to judge income distributions from behind a veil of ignorance, i.e. not knowing their own position in society, and another in which respondents have to judge distributions when they know their own place in society. For the first situation, they refer to Rawls (1971), for the second they refer to Scanlon (1982) who considers negotiating parties that have full knowledge of their personal characteristics as well as economic and social circumstances and have equal bargaining power. Even in the latter case, individuals are likely not to follow just their pure self-interest, because the other group members or contracting parties would then have reasonable arguments to reject the proposed agreement.

Individual participants were allocated randomly into the two experimental treatments. In each group of five, individual positions within the income distribution were assigned by a random mechanism, where each student had a 1/5 chance of ending up in each of the five income classes. In the veil of ignorance treatment (VI), students did not know their income classes at the time when they made their choices. In the no veil of ignorance version (NVI), students knew their income classes at the time of their choices. The participants were informed that they would earn money depending on their own income class in the experiment and on the income distribution on which their group agreed. If there were no unanimous choice, each member of the group would receive 6 euros. So each group member had veto power over the choice of the group. Individual choices were not made public so that anonymity was preserved in the case of a non-unanimous group decision.

The results show that the alteration of the choice set or the order of alternative distributions within a choice set did not have an effect on group choices. Both the utilitarian distribution and the range-constraint distribution were not very popular under either treatment. However, the truly surprising point is that Rawlsian choices were made more frequently without the veil than behind the veil. More concretely, behind the veil 62% of the students chose the distribution with the floor constraint; only 14% made a choice according to Rawls. In the NVI situation, 60% of the participants made a decision according to Rawls, while 20% voted for the floor-constraint variant.

The decision in favour of the floor constraint behind the veil is in line with the results in Frohlich *et al.* (1987). But how to explain the results for the NVI? Herne and Suojanen see a conflict of interest between self-interested choices and fairness. The authors had asked their students at the end of the experiment to name arguments that were exchanged among the members of their group. They report that justice was the most often given argument in the NVI version. Moreover, equality of the income distribution was used as an argument more often in the NVI treatment than in the VI treatment. On the other hand, the most frequently given argument in the VI treatment was a compromise between maximization and equality. Therefore, the authors infer that the NVI scenario was more likely to generate arguments related to justice and equality than the VI scenario. This is quite surprising as a verdict, since it seems to be in stark opposition to the Rawlsian reasoning.[18] Yet, it is perfectly in line with the doubts about the 'veil of ignorance' concept that were raised by the results from the questionnaire studies described in section 3.3.

Both Frohlich *et al.* (1987) and Herne and Suojanen (2004) introduced group decision-making in their experimental setup. This is not a fully adequate representation of the individual decision-making problem that lies at the heart of the 'veil of ignorance' approach. In their experiment, Traub *et al.* (2005) depart from the idea of group discussions. They investigate the evaluation of income distributions by an individual respondent for two different roles in which that evaluating person may find herself, and for two different information scenarios. The two roles are that of an outside observer with no stakes, called an umpire, and that of a person who becomes an income recipient within her most favoured income distribution, once the veil of ignorance has been lifted, called the self-concern mode. Note that these two roles are similar to the H1 and H2 treatments in the questionnaire study of Amiel *et al.* (2009), or the ISO and VOI treatments in Bosmans and Schokkaert (2004). The two informational scenarios in Traub *et al.* (2005) are the case of 'ignorance', where it is assumed that only the set of possible incomes is known, while there is absolutely no information on probabilities, and the case of 'risk', where agents know both the possible incomes and the probability distribution over these incomes. The former (ignorance) scenario was devised to mimic the Rawlsian setup, in which the difference principle is derived without using the concept of probability. The latter (risk) scenario was designed to mimic the Harsanyi-type environment that we discussed in section 3.3.

Combining the self-concern mode and the umpire mode with the two scenarios of ignorance and risk gives four different situations. The authors wanted the students to participate in all four cases. The

---

[18] One should keep in mind, though, that in the present experiment with income distributions the issue was not to agree on the basic structure of society which was Rawls' particular focus.

experiment lasted for two hours. There were material incentives for the students which depended on their choices in the course of the experiment; 61 students were involved in this study, mostly from economics and business administration. The authors assert that there were no gender differences in the students' responses. It appears as if the sequence in which the four cases were given to the students was not varied among the participants. So it was not possible to check for order effects – for example, learning.

The ignorance scenario, depicted in Table 3.14, consisted of nine income sets. These sets represented eligible entries in income distributions. Respondents were told that the eventual income distributions were made up by using components of these sets but that not all components of these sets necessarily entered the ensuing income distribution. This was said in order to destroy any connotation of probabilities. The risk scenario, shown in Table 3.15, consisted of twelve income distributions, each of which contained exactly five entries representing income quintiles. In all twelve distributions, agents knew both the possible incomes and their probability distributions.

Table 3.14. *Income sets in the ignorance scenario*

No.	Income set
1	{59,000 110,000}
2	{60,000}
3	{40,000 45,000 50,000 55,000 60,000}
4	{30,000 150,000}
5	{30,000 180,000}
6	{20,000 50,000 100,000 150,000 220,000}
7	{20,000 60,000 100,000 160,000 220,000}
8	{0 100,000 220,000 250,000}
9	{10,000 20,000 30,000 40,000 45,000 50,000 55,000 60,000 80,000 90,000 100,000}

Table 3.15. *Income distributions in the risk scenario*

No.	Income distribution
1	{60,000 60,000 60,000 60,000 60,000}
2	{50,000 55,000 60,000 65,000 70,000}
3	{40,000 50,000 60,000 70,000 80,000}
4	{40,000 40,000 60,000 80,000 80,000}
5	{40,000 60,000 60,000 60,000 80,000}
6	{10,000 20,000 60,000 100,000 110,000}
7	{10,000 60,000 60,000 60,000 110,000}
8	{70,000 70,000 100,000 110,000 120,000}
9	{70,000 70,000 70,000 90,000 180,000}
10	{15,000 15,000 100,000 110,000 120,000}
11	{15,000 15,000 70,000 90,000 180,000}
12	{0 60,000 80,000 250,000 250,000}

The respondents were required to state complete preference orderings both over the nine income sets in the ignorance scenario and the twelve income distributions in the risk scenario. In the analysis of their results, Traub *et al.* (2005) did not only investigate differences in the respondents' behaviour under the self-concern mode and under the mode of an external observer. They also checked whether and to what degree the respondents' orderings came close to theoretical principles, such as the Rawlsian maximin principle or its lexicographic variant, Harsanyi's utilitarian criterion, or the hybrid standard of maximization of expected utility with a floor constraint, which they call Boulding's principle.

Table 3.16 gives an overview of the rankings by the students of the nine income sets for the ignorance scenario under both the self-concern mode and the umpire mode. Under the self-concern mode, income set 7 was ranked highest with income set 6 winning the second position (note that set 7 weakly vector-dominates set 6). Income set 8,

Table 3.16. *Mean rank and students' rankings of income sets in the ignorance scenario*

	Income set	Self-concern		Umpire	
No.	(× 1000)	Mean rank	Ranking position	Mean rank	Ranking position
1	{59, 110}	4.11	3	4.25	3
2	{60}	5.51	5	4.70	5
3	{40, 45, 50, 55, 60}	5.92	7	6.64	9
4	{30, 150}	5.93	8	5.49	7
5	{30, 180}	5.07	4	5.07	6
6	{20, 50, 100, 150, 220}	3.48	2	4.15	2
7	{20, 60, 100, 160, 220}	2.92	1	3.92	1
8	{0, 100, 220, 250}	6.16	9	4.51	4
9	{10, 20, 30, 40, 45, 50, 55, 60, 80, 90, 100}	5.90	6	6.28	8

where one of the incomes is zero, fared very badly. Under the umpire mode, sets 7 and 6 were still at the top but they lost in terms of mean rank. Interestingly, income set 8 gained five rank positions. Subjects, in their role as outside observer, seem to have thought that the possibility of rather high incomes under set 8 compensates the society for the chance of a zero income. 'However, when possibly affected by a zero income under the self-concern mode, they shied away from income set 8' (Traub *et al.*, 2005, p. 296).

To evaluate the 'performance' of the various theoretical principles, the authors computed the theoretical ranking of the nine income sets for each principle. Then, for every respondent, Spearman's rank correlation between the respondent's empirical rank ordering of the nine income sets and any theoretical ranking was computed. The authors report that under the self-concern mode,

Boulding's principle and expected utility were among the winning standards of behaviour and both were also in the leading group under the umpire mode. The leximin principle was the big loser under both modes. Furthermore, the authors observed a shift in the respondents' assessment of the income sets when switching from self-concern to external observer. On average, respondents behaved less inequality-averse under the umpire mode than under the self-concern mode. This means that if a utilitarian structure was underlying the respondents' evaluations, the shape of the utility function became less concave for the external observer. Remember also that income set 8, with the possibility of a zero income, made a big jump from the self-concern to the umpire mode, obviously suggesting a lower degree of inequality aversion among a larger subgroup of the students in the latter case. Simple conclusions would be too rash, however, since 23% of the students behaved more inequality-averse as umpires.

In Table 3.17, the mean ranks and the students' rankings of the income distributions in the risk scenario are given. When switching from self-concern to external observer, the income distributions 8, 9 and 12, characterized by high payoff, high risk and high variance lose significantly in mean rank in favour of the distributions 1, 3, 4 and 5, which have low payoffs, low risk and low variance. The figures therefore suggest that the respondents, on average, exhibited more inequality aversion under the umpire role than under self-concern. These results for the risk scenario are consistent with the overall pattern found in the questionnaire study of Amiel et al. (2009). But also in the present case, one should be cautious. Although income distributions 8 and 9 have lost in terms of mean rank when going from self-concern to umpire, they still rank highest in the students' orderings. Interestingly, for income distribution 12, which contains a zero income, one observes a reaction which is in total contrast to the one for income set 8 in the ignorance scenario.

A statistical analysis analogous to the one briefly outlined in connection with the ignorance scenario shows that, again, expected utility maximization is among the winning standards of behaviour.

Table 3.17. *Mean rank and students' rankings of income distributions in the risk scenario*

No.	Income distribution	Self-concern Mean rank	Ranking position	Umpire Mean rank	Ranking position
1	(60, 60, 60, 60, 60)	6.95	5	5.62	3
2	(50, 55, 60, 65, 70)	6.66	4	6.28	5
3	(40, 50, 60, 70, 80)	7.61	9	6.41	6
4	(40, 40, 60, 80, 80)	7.79	10	6.77	8
5	(40, 60, 60, 60, 80)	7.30	8	6.08	4
6	(10, 20, 60, 100, 110)	9.02	12	9.03	12
7	(10, 60, 60, 60, 110)	8.46	11	7.75	11
8	(70, 70, 100, 110, 120)	2.48	1	4.15	1
9	(70, 70, 70, 90, 180)	2.59	2	4.34	2
10	(15, 15, 100, 110, 120)	7.07	6	7.46	9
11	(15, 15, 70, 90, 180)	7.11	7	7.59	10
12	(0, 60, 80, 250, 250)	4.98	3	6.51	7

The Boulding principle fares 'relatively well' under the umpire mode. Leximin behaviour fares much better now than under the ignorance scenario, though it is 'quite far away' from expected utility maximization. Finally, an estimation of the values of the inequality aversion parameter confirms that in the role of an umpire, the students showed a higher degree of inequality aversion than under the self-concern mode. In other words, the shape of the utility function became more concave for the external observer.

The Traub *et al.* (2005) study gives some additional support for the popularity of the Boulding principle in an experimental setting. Their results in the risk scenario are largely coherent with the questionnaire studies from section 3.3, in that an outside observer seems to be more inequality averse than a self-concerned decision-maker behind a veil of ignorance. However, in the ignorance scenario where no probability information was available, a larger group of respondents was more inequality-averse when they were personally affected by the realization of a particular income distribution. The reasons for the difference between the two scenarios are not altogether clear so that the reader feels rather left in doubt. Two aspects within the Traub *et al.* (2005) investigation appear somewhat problematic. In the first place, the student sample was relatively small in comparison to most other studies ($n = 61$) and, secondly, all participants had to 'play' two roles on two occasions, viz. be self-concerned and be an umpire. Can the human mind easily switch between those two roles?

3.4.2 Questionnaire studies

The experimental results described in subsection 3.4.1 confirm that the concept of the 'veil of ignorance' is far from evident and that the link between decisions in a hypothetical risky situation and ethical judgments is fragile. Yet, what to think about the remarkably robust popularity of utilitarianism with a floor constraint? The experimental designs of Frohlich *et al.* (1987) and Herne and Suojanen (2004) have some specific features that may partly explain their result. While in most questionnaire studies there is no explicit enumeration of principles, in these studies students were first introduced to the alternative principles of distributive justice which they were then asked to rank. Moreover, subjects were given a chance to discuss these principles and then to collectively choose a particular one. Consensus within a group was beneficial for the individual group members in terms of payments to be earned in the course of the experiment. So there was a clear incentive to reach an agreement within each group (which then reflected the group's preference). It is doubtful that this setting induces impartial reasoning on the part of the participating students, which is the basic objective of the questionnaire studies. Having said this, the results of Herne and Suojanen (2004) when the veil was totally lifted are the more surprising. Moreover, the Boulding principle remained rather popular in the setup of Traub *et al.* (2005) in which group discussions did not take place. Does utilitarianism with a floor also come out prominently in questionnaire studies that aim to test for it directly?

A first relevant study is that by Faravelli (2007). We focus on one of his scenarios in which the aspect of needs is predominant, and that he himself uses to shed some light on the principle of utilitarianism with a floor. This situation is as follows:

Q 3.15: After a shipwreck Robinson and Friday have landed on two different islands divided by a narrow but deep channel. On each of the two islands one can till 12 plants. The only reason why both Robinson and Friday would like to cultivate these plants is because they produce fruit and the higher amount of fruit they obtain, the more their welfare would be; every additional fruit produces an equal value, which is identical for both people. It has been decided that you are the one who will choose how to distribute the plants between Robinson and Friday. You have been given the following information, which the two survivors also know:

The minimum quantity needed by every one of them in order to survive is 300 fruits per year.

Robinson lives on island *A* and Friday lives on island *B*.

All plants of one island are identical to the ones of the other island. How much fruit they produce depends on the way they are cultivated.

Friday obtains 120 fruits per year from every plant on island *B*, but he cannot obtain any fruit from island *A*'s plants.

On both islands Robinson obtains 20 fruits per plant.

There is no possibility of redistributing the plants after the allocation and there is also no chance to exchange any fruit which is produced.

How would you divide the 12 plants of island *A* and the 12 plants of island *B* so that, from your point of view, the distribution would be just? Choose:

1	Plants island A	Plants island B	Fruits
Robinson	12	0	240
Friday	0	12	1,440
Total production of fruits			1,680
2	Plants island A	Plants island B	Fruits
Robinson	12	8	400
Friday	0	4	480
Total production of fruits			880
3	Plants island A	Plants island B	Fruits
Robinson	9	9	360
Friday	3	3	360
Total production of fruits			720
4	Plants island A	Plants island B	Fruits
Robinson	12	3	300
Friday	0	9	1,080
Total production of fruits			1,380

If the minimum quantity needed to survive is interpreted as the floor and utilitarianism is interpreted as maximizing total production (given the assumptions about the welfare of the individuals), the four options coincide with the utilitarian, the Rawlsian, the egalitarian and the Boulding (utilitarian with a floor) solutions, respectively. Note that the respondents are put in the shoes of an outside observer.

This situation was given to 418 students of the University of Milan in 2002. These were economics freshers, economics seniors, sociology freshers and sociology seniors. The students were asked to choose a solution among the ones that were provided so that the

Table 3.18. *Results of Faravelli (2007): needs case*

Solutions	Economics freshers	Economics seniors	Sociology freshers	Sociology seniors
Egalitarian	30	19	41	36
Rawlsian	40	44	44	31
Utilitarian	4	1	0	3
Utilitarian with floor	26	36	15	30

distribution was considered just. The answers (expressed in percentages) are given in Table 3.18.

Egalitarianism seems to be the preferred principle among sociology students though its popularity decreases from first-year sociology students to seniors in favour of utilitarianism with a floor. Among economics students, the Rawlsian principle is the most popular, utilitarianism with a floor is second and 'pure' utilitarianism fares very badly. This last statement is a bit unfair since the utilitarian solution does not guarantee the minimum provision of fruit for survival so that it is unacceptable *per se* for almost all respondents. However, in a comparison between utilitarianism with a floor and Rawlsianism, the clear-cut experimental results in the wake of Frohlich *et al.* (1987) are by no means substantiated. Table 3.18 shows that, while utilitarianism with a constraint fares quite well, Rawlsian maximin does even better, among both economics and sociology students. The relative popularity of maximin in this setting with needs echoes the results of Yaari and Bar-Hillel (1984) that were described at the very beginning of this chapter (pp. 35–6).

Another relevant study is Schwettmann (2008), who focuses explicitly on what he calls 'truncated efficiency', where the truncation again refers to a floor constraint. His base situation goes as follows:

Q 3.16: Imagine two almost equal settlements, *A* and *B*, far in the North. For the last time before the annual closure of their ports in

winter, both villages can be reached by a tankship. The cargo
capacity of the only available ship is restricted to 70,000 litres. Both
settlements need diesel fuel for both the operation of their respective
saw mill and the heating of residential houses. The mills are the only
income source of the inhabitants of both villages, who otherwise live
at subsistence level.

Settlement A has already enough fuel available for heating.
Moreover, the stock suffices for a daily two-hour operation of the
saw mill. Each additional 10,000 litres of fuel would allow for
operating the mill for 1 more hour per day.

Settlement B has no available reserve of diesel fuel, because the
shipping company, which was commissioned to deliver 40,000 litres
of fuel in autumn, declared itself bankrupt. This quantity would be
necessary to heat the residential houses in settlement B during the
whole winter period. A smaller quantity would leave all houses
unheated for some time. If settlement B received an additional quantity
of fuel, an operation of the saw mill would also be possible. The
operation of the mill for 1 hour per day requires 20,000 litres of fuel.

Please state now how much of the 70,000 litres of fuel the
tankship should deliver to each settlement. You may either pick one
of the given allocations or state your own alternative in the last
column:

Settlement A (000 litres)	70	35	30	20	15	10	5	0	...
Settlement B (000 litres)	0	35	40	50	55	60	65	70	...
Your choice:	□	□	□	□	□	□	□	□	□

Out of the various solutions proposed to the students, the allocation (30,40) can be interpreted as utilitarianism with the fulfilment
of basic needs in settlement B (note that settlement A is twice as
efficient as settlement B). The solution (10,60) represents the decision
to fulfil basic needs in B and equate additional benefits. Since it violates the principle of efficiency, it cannot be characterized as utilitarianism with a threshold. The solution (0,70) is the maximin allocation.

The participants in Schwettmann's (2008) study were 205 undergraduate students in economics and business administration at the University of Osnabrück. He found that only 5.9% of his sample supported truncated efficiency, i.e. utilitarianism with a floor; 46.1% voted for the fulfilment of basic needs plus an equalization of additional benefits and 30.4% supported the maximin allocation. So, again, efficiency with a lower bound does not fare too well. The maximin allocation in fact gets much more support from the respondents.

Schwettmann had another scenario in which an aspect of responsibility was introduced. In that scenario, 'settlement B does not have available any reserve of diesel fuel, because the inhabitants used up the required 40,000 litres of fuel as a result of already wasting energy in autumn'. In this variant, truncated efficiency becomes much more acceptable (going up to 21.4%) and, at the same time, maximin loses much support (down to 6.8%). Responsibility apparently is a crucial issue in fairness judgments and we will discuss it extensively in Chapter 4. However, it was not present in the experimental settings described above and can therefore not explain the differences between the results in the experiments and in the questionnaire studies. In still another Schwettmann scenario, the productive efficiency in settlement A was significantly increased. In that case, maximin did not lose much support. The support of truncated efficiency grew substantially but remained much weaker than the support for maximin. We will return to the issue of efficiency in section 3.5.

3.5 THE PARETO PRINCIPLE

Economists tend to interpret efficiency in terms of the Pareto principle. A situation is called 'Pareto-efficient' if it is not possible to improve the situation of at least one individual without harming at least one other person. Pareto efficiency is a universally accepted criterion within (welfare) economics. Indeed, at first sight it seems rather evident that a movement from some given allocation to another should be preferred if it provides more for at least one person while keeping everybody else at the same level. But do respondents really accept this principle when they realize that some other person gets more while they themselves do not experience any improvement? And do they take into account this kind of consideration when they are in the position of an outside ethical observer? We first present an experimental study designed to answer the first question and then introduce a questionnaire study relevant to the second one.

Like the experiments in section 3.4, Beckman *et al.* (2002) start from the contrast between economic decisions made when positions in society are known and decisions taken under impersonal circumstances. They exploit this setting, however, in order to isolate the impacts of what they call envy and malice. They argue that ignoring envy and malice neglects 'significant factors motivating economic decisions involving more than one person' (2002, p. 352).

The experiment was run in the US, Russia, Taiwan and the People's Republic (PR) of China. There are four groups of 10 subjects each in all four countries, giving a total of 160 subjects. The 40 participants in China were asked to take part in the entire experiment twice, once at low and once at high pay levels. Students were randomly divided into two groups of five at the beginning of the experiment. There were seven rounds. In each round, the experimenter shuffles five cards, ace through five, fans them out face down and walks before each subject in the group of five who then points to a card which is placed face up in front of him or her. This card determines the position within the possible payoff vectors.

The payoff table that was provided to each participant before the experiment started is reproduced in Table 3.19. Vector *B* always represents a Pareto improvement. In the first five rounds, 30 points are added to positions 5, 4, 3, 2 and 1, respectively. Round 6 adds 300 points to position 5 and is used to test support for large increases in pay for the person in the highest position. Round 7 redistributes income slightly compared to round 6 as 20 points are taken from the potential gain to position 5 and divided equally among the four remaining positions. Rounds 6 and 7 were used to determine whether allowing every participant to have at least a small gain would offset opposition

Table 3.19. *Payoff table (Beckman* et al., *2002)*

Round/Vote	Position assigned by distributing five cards				
	Ace	Two	Three	Four	Five
1A	40	80	120	160	200
B	40	80	120	160	230
2A	40	80	120	160	200
B	40	80	120	190	200
3A	40	80	120	160	200
B	40	80	150	160	200
4A	40	80	120	160	200
B	40	110	120	160	200
5A	40	80	120	160	200
B	70	80	120	160	200
6A	40	80	120	160	200
B	40	80	120	160	500
7A	40	80	120	160	200
B	45	85	125	165	480

to Pareto optimality that benefits only the highest position. All points gained were later converted at a particular rate into local currencies.

Each participant votes for vector *A* or *B* or abstains. In all experiments, the set of payoff vectors is used twice. The only difference between the two sets is whether voting occurs before or after cards have been distributed. Half the experiments begin with voting before cards are distributed and half with voting after cards are handed out. The experimenter registers the vote and announces the majority decision that determines which vector is used for payoffs. If there is a tie, a coin is tossed to determine the outcome. After registering all data, the next round begins.

Table 3.20. *Results of experiment (Beckman et al., 2002): part I*

| Definition | % of votes | | | % of obs. |
| | Oppose | Support | Abstain | |
	Pareto improvements			
Full sample of 2,800 votes	15.4	78.6	6.0	100
Data collected in US	6.4	91.0	2.5	20
Data collected in PR China	20.0	73.8	6.2	40
Data collected in Russia	21.4	73.8	4.8	20
Data collected in Taiwan	9.1	80.2	10.7	20
Data from the high pay exp. in PR China	19.1	75.7	5.2	20
Subjects know their position before voting	20.6	69.4	10.0	50
Subjects vote not knowing positions	10.1	87.7	2.1	50
Recipient's position is above the voter	28.8	59.3	11.9	26
Recipient's position is below the voter	18.3	69.2	12.5	14
Recipient of Pareto gain is the voter	3.2	95.4	1.4	10
Data from round 7 and positions known	10.0	87.0	3.0	7
Data from round 6 and positions known	30.5	61.0	8.5	7

Tables 3.20 and 3.21 present the overall statistics for the full sample of 2,800 votes (200 × 7 × 2). The last column in Table 3.20 gives the percentage of observations involved. To give an example: the sum of the percentages of 'Recipient's position is above the voter', 'Recipient's position is below the voter' and 'Recipient of Pareto gain is the voter' equals 50, as these situations are obviously

Table 3.21. *Results of experiment (Beckman et al., 2002): part II*

	China	High pay	Russia	Taiwan	US	All
	% of opposition to Pareto optimality					
Rounds 1–5						
Behind veil	14.0	6.0	21.5	5.5	8.0	11.0
Positions known	29.5	30.0	24.0	14.5	6.0	20.8
Self	2.5	7.5	7.5	0.0	0.0	3.5
Above	43.8	47.5	36.3	20.0	12.5	32.0
Below	28.8	23.8	20.0	16.3	2.5	18.3
Round 6						
Behind veil	12.5	7.5	20.0	5.0	2.5	9.5
Positions known	32.5	55.0	32.5	17.5	15.0	30.5
Self	0.0	12.5	12.5	0.0	0.0	5.0
Above	40.6	65.6	37.5	21.9	18.8	36.9
Round 7						
Behind veil	10.0	5.0	12.5	5.0	0.0	6.5
Positions known	20.0	20.0	7.5	0.0	2.5	10.0
Self	0.0	0.0	0.0	0.0	0.0	0.0
Above	25.0	25.0	9.4	0.0	3.1	12.5
All						
Behind veil	13.2	6.1	20.0	5.4	6.1	10.1
Positions known	28.6	32.1	22.9	12.9	6.8	20.6

only distinguishable in the information treatment, i.e. in half of the experiments.

Across nations, only 10.1% oppose Pareto improvements when positions are not known. However, opposition to Pareto gains increases to 18.3% when the recipient of this gain is, income-wise, below the voter (a case of malice) and it is 28.8% when the recipient occupies a higher income position than the voter (a case of envy). There are large differences across countries. In the US, opposition to a Pareto gain is only 6.4%; in Taiwan 9.1%; in China and Russia, however, opposition lies between 20% and 21.4%. We will come back to the interpretation and the relevance of these international differences in Chapter 6. It is interesting to note that in China, the differences between the 'normal-pay' and 'high-pay' level are only minor in the case where the positions are known. A comparison between the data from rounds 6 and 7 shows that, in the case where positions are known, the overall opposition against a Pareto gain falls from 30.5% in round 6 to only 10% in round 7. A widespread participation in Pareto gains, even if it is only of a minimal kind, generates broad support.

A multinomial logit model shows that knowing the position of who on the income scale receives the Pareto gain (the voter, an individual above, a person below) is highly significant (at the 1% level). Support for a Pareto gain is stronger when the voter is the recipient, and it becomes weaker in the other case. Moreover, the support for gains going to someone higher in the distribution is less than support for gains to someone lower in the distribution. The difference between these two effects is statistically significant. Turned around, the evidence for envy appears to be stronger than that for malice. So the relative position matters. Acceptance of the Pareto criterion is not universal.

The relevance of envy (and the rejection of Pareto efficiency) is also found in other experimental settings. As an example, Klemisch-Ahlert (1992) shows in her bargaining experiments that envy may generate payoff agreements that are not strongly Pareto-optimal. The rejection of the Pareto criterion is also quite common in questionnaire studies. It was already reported by McClelland and Rohrbaugh (1978). Another illustration is offered by Konow (2001). He asks the following question given to a sample of students:

Q 3.17A: A small newly independent island nation is considering how to allocate its one banana plantation and its one sugar plantation. There are only two farmers in the island interested in these plantations. The government chooses among the following two plans either of which would result in the same total production of both bananas and sugar.

Plan X: Both farmers receive one-half of each plantation. Each farmer earns an average profit of US $100 per day from bananas and sugar combined. Therefore, the total of both farmers' profits is US $200 per day.

Plan Y: One farmer receives the banana plantation and the other farmer receives the sugar plantation. The average daily profit of the banana farmer is US $150 and that of the sugar farmer is also US $150. At US $300 per day, combined profits are greater under this plan because specialization reduces production costs.

Please circle the plan that you consider more fair.

Another sample of students receives a variant of Q 3.17A. The change is in the formulation of plan Y, which now reads as:

Q 3.17B: Plan Y: One farmer receives the banana plantation and the other farmer receives the sugar plantation. The farmers' profits are unequal since the sugar plantation is more profitable than the banana plantation: average daily profit of the banana farmer is US $100 and that of the sugar farmer is US $200. At US $300 per day, combined profits are greater under this plan because specialization reduces production costs.

Please circle the plan that you consider more fair.

Note that in both variants plan Y is more efficient, in that it generates larger combined profits. Moreover, in both cases none of the farmers has lower profits under Y than under X. However, in variant B the profits are unequally distributed, while their distribution is equal under variant A. This turns out to have a very strong effect on the answers of the respondents, as shown in Table 3.22.

In version A the efficiency gain for farmers due to a specialization in production is widely acknowledged by the respondents. Plan Y is by far the most popular. In version B, however, where only one farmer earns larger profits in Y than in X, while the other remains at the same

Table 3.22. *Acceptance of productive efficiency*

	Plan X (% of respondents)	Plan Y (% of respondents)
Variant A (n = 147)	20	80
Variant B (n = 132)	57	43

level, a majority of the respondents opts for plan X, where the combined profits are lower but equally distributed. The sharp fall in the support for Plan Y is stunning, given that plan X is not Pareto-efficient. Konow (2001) interprets this finding as resulting from a conflict between Pareto efficiency and what he calls the 'accountability' principle. The formulation of Q 3.17B indeed strongly suggests that the banana farmer cannot be held responsible for the lower profitability of his plantation. We will return to the responsibility issue and to Konow's notion of accountability in Chapter 4. For present purposes, it is sufficient to emphasize that the rather intuitive (as economists often say) Pareto efficiency criterion is not that cherished by respondents after all. Equality may be pursued at the cost of efficiency.[19]

There is one important caveat, however. If envy and/or malice are at stake (as was strongly suggested by the experiment in Beckman et al., 2002), these can be seen as externalities in the utility function. It is then possible to reconcile the choice for X in Konow's variant B with a respect for Pareto efficiency in the space of utilities, because the unequal distribution of profits may generate a utility loss for the banana farmer. And, possibly, the evaluations of the respondents as outside observers will have been guided by such a utility function. This is corroborated by Amiel and Cowell (1994). While they also find large opposition to what they call 'monotonicity' (unilateral

---

[19] In some other scenarios, Konow (2001) has also checked for the acceptance of the Kaldor–Hicks compensation principle. The idea of hypothetical compensation does not get much support from the students.

income increases), they argue that the overall pattern of responses suggests that the problem does not lie in the Pareto criterion *per se* but rather in the assumption that utility is dependent only on one's own income. We should therefore be rather cautious in using the results from this section as a conclusive argument against the concept of Pareto efficiency.

3.6 CONCLUSION

Empirical studies have yielded some interesting insights into prominent issues within the traditional framework of social choice. Respondents are willing to compensate for differences in needs. The maximin criterion turns out to be (surprisingly?) popular in this context. However, the support for the equity axiom is not unconditional. If the efficiency losses become too large, many respondents will take them into account in their evaluations. The impartial judgments of an outside ethical observer apparently do not coincide with the choices made by a concerned individual behind a veil of ignorance. This raises deep questions on the ethical relevance of the whole concept of the veil of ignorance. More specifically, while utilitarianism with a floor constraint turns out to be quite popular in experiments that mimic a hypothetical original position, it is much less supported by outside ethical observers in questionnaire studies. In fact, in the latter studies there is greater support for maximin. Different studies have shown that the relative position in the income distribution seems to matter for respondents and may induce envy or malice. These externalities even lead to a common rejection of income increases for a subset of individuals, if the income situation of the others does not change. The Pareto criterion is rejected in its simplistic interpretation, in which utility depends on one's own income only.

The most crucial insight from the questionnaire studies is probably a negative one. It appears that the traditional welfarist framework is not sufficient to capture all the intuitions of the respondents. The results of Yaari and Bar-Hillel (1984) strongly suggest that respondents react differently to scenarios which should be equivalent from a welfarist perspective. Respondents distinguish between needs and tastes and discount subjective beliefs to a large extent. In general, intuitions about distributive justice seem to depend on the context in which the problem is formulated. Moreover, the issue of responsibility, which is largely absent in the traditional social choice framework, has cropped up already a couple of times in our description of results. In a certain sense, these empirical findings can be seen as a corroboration of the important recent trend in social choice theory away from the simple welfarist framework. Some of these new developments will be the topic of Chapter 4.

The results in this chapter have also sharpened some of the methodological issues that were already touched upon in Chapter 2. How to explain international and intertemporal differences in ethical judgments? More importantly, how to reconcile them with the quest for a universal theory of justice? Why is the principle of utilitarianism with a floor constraint more popular in an experimental laboratory than in the questionnaire studies? Does this reveal something about the differences between these two settings? Which of the two is more relevant for empirical social choice? These broader issues will be further discussed in Chapter 6.

4 New questions: fairness in economic environments

We have seen in Chapter 3 that, according to many empirical studies, information on individual welfare levels alone does not suffice to capture the moral intricacies of real-world distribution problems. Recent developments in social choice theory also depart from the traditional welfarist assumptions. Overly simplifying, one could say that these new approaches have some common characteristics. Many authors working in the area reject the meaningfulness of interpersonal utility comparisons. They try to introduce into their formal models the necessary information that is missing in the more traditional approach. As they accept that justice or fairness evaluations may depend on the economic and social context, they formulate their problems within a richer description of the economic environment. This richness implies going beyond utility information. Solutions and decision rules are often derived within the axiomatic setting of cooperative game theory. At the same time there is a strong and growing interest in incentive compatibility and in mechanism design, and an intensive search for non-cooperative foundations of cooperative solutions. In many models the concept of individual responsibility plays a crucial role, although it can be defined in different ways.

In spite of the fact that these theoretical developments have taken place independently of the questionnaire studies, some of the work that was described in Chapter 3 (notably Yaari and Bar-Hillel, 1984) has been influential in strengthening the motivation to look for new approaches. Moreover, empirical social choice, as we define it, has probably a more important role to play in these new approaches than in traditional social choice. The 'new' axioms and solution concepts often relate to everyday intuitions. It is easier to construct cases that fit a rich description of the economic environment than to formulate questions at the highly abstract level of Arrovian social choice theory. Moreover, there really is room for choice. Different sets of axioms, often incompatible across sets, lead to different theoretically equally respectable solutions and it is not clear which of these axioms or solutions come closest to the ethical judgments of citizens. However, the empirical work has just started and much remains to be done. In this chapter we will focus on the few questions that have already been analysed to some extent. We will first discuss the different interpretations of individual responsibility and the way it has been taken up in the formal models. We will then focus on one interesting example of a specific distributive issue: the claims (or estate division) problem. Finally, we will comment on the differences between dividing benefits versus harms. Chapter 5 will be devoted to applications in one specific domain, that of health. Non-welfarist approaches have been prominent in health economics from the very beginning and Chapter 5 is therefore a natural continuation of Chapter 4.

Before moving on, we would like to emphasize that all this does *not* mean that the analyses from Chapter 3 have lost their relevance. First, the debate on welfarism has not yet been resolved and social welfare functions are still the dominating approach in public economics. Second, basic philosophical debates such as the one around the veil of ignorance also crop up in non-welfarist social choice. One of the most prominent examples is the work of Dworkin, who in the first of two very influential articles (Dworkin, 1981a) rejects welfarism and in the second (Dworkin, 1981b) proposes a non-welfarist alternative in which a (reinterpreted) concept of the veil of ignorance plays an essential role. Third, some of the principles and axioms that have been discussed in Chapter 3 also remain relevant in the new fairness approaches. This is certainly true for the Pareto principle and for the equity axiom.

4.1   RESPONSIBILITY-SENSITIVE EGALITARIANISM
Many authors have argued that the desire to reward effort is an important component of the common-sense conception of justice (see, e.g.,

Elster, 1992) and the same idea is at the core of so-called desert-based theories of justice (such as that of Miller, 1976). 'Equity theory', one of the most important theories of distributive justice in psychology and sociology (Adams, 1965, Homans, 1958, Walster *et al.*, 1973) stated in its original form that inputs (into a relationship) and outputs (out of a relationship) should be in the same proportion for all persons involved. In many practical applications inputs are related to effort and a lot of empirical work has tested and to some extent confirmed the theory.

Within empirical social choice, the crucial importance of effort for fairness judgments was already found by Schokkaert and Capeau (1991) and Schokkaert and Overlaet (1989). It was integrated in a broader approach by Konow (1996, 2001) who argued that one should distinguish between discretionary and exogenous variables. A discretionary variable affects output and can be controlled or influenced by the person considered (e.g. work effort). An exogenous variable can have an influence on the amount or quality of output but cannot, under normal circumstances, be influenced by the person (e.g. some physical disability). Konow then proposed a so-called 'accountability principle', calling for allocations to be in proportion to volitional contributions, meaning that 'a worker who is twice as productive as another should be paid twice as much if the higher productivity is due to greater work effort but not if it is due to innate aptitude' (Konow, 2001, p. 138). Thus, Konow argues, 'individuals are only held accountable for factors they may reasonably control' (2001, p. 142). The relationship with equity theory is obvious.

Do respondents share this view? Konow gave the following question plus variations to students at his university:

Q 4.1: Bob and John are identical in terms of physical and mental abilities. They become shipwrecked on an uninhabited island where the only food is bananas. They can collect as many bananas as they want by climbing up a tree, picking them before they fall into the ocean and throwing them into a pile. In this way, Bob picks 12 bananas per day and John picks 8 per day. Bob takes from the pile the

12 bananas he picked leaving John with the 8 that John picked.
Please rate this as fair or unfair.

A first variant (Q 4.2) has exactly the same background, but a different
description of the abilities of Bob and John. A third variant (Q 4.3) is
identical to Q 4.2 except for the proposed division of the output. The
relevant parts of these questions read as follows:

Q 4.2: Bob and John are identical in terms of physical and mental
abilities except that Bob was born with one hand and John with two.
Together they pick a total of 20 bananas per day, but because of his
condition Bob picks fewer bananas per day than John. John takes 12
bananas from the pile leaving 8 for Bob. Please rate this as fair or
unfair.

Q 4.3: Bob and John are identical in terms of physical and mental
abilities except that Bob was born with one hand and John with two.
Together they pick a total of 20 bananas per day, but because of his
condition Bob picks fewer bananas per day than John. John takes
10 bananas from the pile leaving 10 for Bob. Please rate this as fair or
unfair.

The results (in percentages) are given in Table 4.1. They offer very
strong support for the idea of accountability. In the initial situation,
i.e. Q 4.1, there are no explicit exogenous differences between the two
persons. The only difference between them is of a discretionary type,
i.e. harvesting bananas. So, according to accountability, Bob should get
12, John should receive 8 bananas. There is a wide agreement among

Table 4.1. *The effect of accountability (Konow, 2001)*

	Q 4.1 ($n = 76$)	Q 4.2 ($n = 78$)	Q 4.3 ($n = 78$)
Fair	74%	19%	90%
Unfair	26%	81%	10%

the respondents to support this view. In Q 4.2, however, the greater productivity of two-handed John is not viewed as sufficient ground for granting him 12 bananas from the pile, leaving only 8 to disabled Bob; 81% of the respondents view the larger share of John as unfair. Since Bob is in no way responsible for his disability, an equal split of the harvest, as suggested in Q 4.3, is seen as fair by an overwhelming majority of the respondents (90%).

Let us now introduce a twist towards larger differences in productivity. The background story is the same as above, but the productivity of one of the two persons is going up sharply, while the second person's productivity is constantly decreasing. This questionnaire study is based on telephone interviews that Konow undertook in the Los Angeles area. The initial question was formulated as follows:

> **Q 4.4**: Bob and John become shipwrecked on an uninhabited island. The only food is bananas which the castaways collect and throw into a pile daily. Bob and John are identical in terms of abilities and work effort except that Bob was born with only one hand and John with two. John picks 14 bananas per day while Bob can pick only 6 because of his condition. John takes 12 bananas from the pile leaving 8 bananas for Bob. Please rate this as fair or unfair.

Note that, differently from Q 4.2, the productivity difference between Bob and John is quantified here. The variants of Q 4.4 are identical, except for the size of the difference in productivities. The relevant changes are:

> **Q 4.5**: (...) John picks 16 bananas per day while Bob can pick only 4 because of his condition. (...)

> **Q 4.6**: (...) John picks 18 bananas per day while Bob can pick only 2 because of his condition. (...)

Note that in all three situations, the total size of the allocable resource is the same. The results (given in Table 4.2) again corroborate the accountability principle in so far as a vast majority in Q 4.4 and still a

Table 4.2. *Increasing the productivity gap (Konow, 2001)*

	Q 4.4 (n = 117)	Q 4.5 (n = 121)	Q 4.6 (n = 109)
Fair	17%	28%	39%
Unfair	83%	72%	61%

large majority in Q 4.5 and Q 4.6 deemed the exogenous differences between Bob and John as irrelevant. However, with John's productivity rising, the opposition against the unequal allocation of 12 bananas for John and 8 for Bob is getting less pronounced. The widening productivity gap is being honoured by a growing group of respondents. This observation is to some degree reminiscent of the results in section 3.2, where students were not willing to compensate Smith for his declining metabolism 'ad infinitum' (Yaari and Bar-Hillel, 1984). Konow makes the conjecture that respondents were, perhaps, worried that if John were not appropriately rewarded for his higher productivity, he might be prompted to scale down his effort which would then reduce the total to be distributed among the two. This second-best argument is not really integrated in his theory, however. Moreover, we have seen already in Chapter 3 that even the Pareto principle is definitely not sacrosanct for respondents if it comes into conflict with fairness considerations.

The results of Konow (2001) show the importance of individual responsibility (his discretionary variables) for fairness judgments. His questions are not strongly rooted in any normative theory, however. In fact, he himself introduces the accountability principle as a 'positive' (or descriptive) theory of economic fairness. It is the more striking that his findings are so closely in line with the recent developments in social choice theory and in political philosophy, on which we will comment later in this section.

Konow's question of responsibility in a setting of basic needs has been further explored by Gaertner and Schwettmann (2007). Contrary to Konow, however, Gaertner and Schwettmann do work within a well-defined formal framework, as they integrate the responsibility issue into their study on the acceptance of the equity axiom. As we saw in section 3.2, when we discussed the situation of the handicapped person and the child(ren), the support for the needy person diminished over the years while efficiency aspects became stronger. Would responsibility as an additionally included argument further reduce the support for the worst-off person?

Gaertner and Schwettmann (2007) formulated two different variants of Q 3.7. In one version, they gave the information that the disabled person was severely handicapped from birth. In a second version, presented to other students, it was said that brain damage was due to an accident from participation in a dangerous sport (paragliding). Otherwise, the descriptions were exactly the same as before. The results are summarized in Table 4.3, which has the same structure as Table 3.4 in Chapter 3. It turns out that fulfilment of the equity axiom is weaker for the responsibility case and, furthermore, that the relative frequency of revising the initial decision is lower in the responsibility version, viz. from 47.2% in the case of handicap from birth to 36.4% in the case of a dangerous sport. Surprisingly, unconditional support for the handicapped (i.e. sequence 0000) was somewhat higher in the latter case than it was in the former. However, the most striking finding is that the overall differences are rather minor. The authors used χ^2 tests to check whether there were statistically significant differences between the answering patterns in the two versions. The null hypothesis that the distribution of responses in the 'responsibility' variant is identical to the distribution in the 'no responsibility' version could not be rejected.

If we compare these results with that of Konow, the effects of introducing differences in individual responsibility are surprisingly small here. In order to learn more about what really was going on, the authors did a gender breakdown. They found that, in comparison with female answers, the fact that the handicap resulted from a sports accident had a positive and significant (at the 5% level) effect on

Table 4.3. *Responsibility and the equity axiom*

				No responsibility 2002 + 2003 $n = 178$	Responsibility 2002 + 2003 $n = 187$
		Sequence			
0	0	0	0	0.360	0.412
0	0	0	1	0.022	0.032
0	0	1	0	0.0	0.0
0	0	1	1	0.213	0.139
0	1	0	0	0.0	0.0
0	1	0	1	0.011	0.0
0	1	1	0	0.006	0.0
0	1	1	1	0.236	0.193
1	0	0	0	0.0	0.0
1	0	0	1	0.0	0.0
1	0	1	0	0.0	0.0
1	0	1	1	0.006	0.011
1	1	0	0	0.011	0.005
1	1	0	1	0.0	0.0
1	1	1	0	0.0	0.0
1	1	1	1	0.135	0.209
% of switch				47.2	36.4
% fulfilment of equity axiom				84.8	77.5

male answers regarding both the fulfilment of the equity axiom and the unconditional support of the worst-off. Having controlled for this effect, there was a highly significant (at the 1% level) negative influence on the fulfilment of the equity axiom coming from female respondents. In other words, basic needs are considerably less often supported by females if the suffering person is to be blamed for her own situation. Perhaps male students to some degree 'honoured' participation in some risky sport, whereas female respondents had a clear reservation about this.[1] This points to a more general crucial difference between the case of Gaertner and Schwettmann (2007) and that of Konow (2001), in that the former takes up the issue of risk and responsibility for risk. Not all paragliders have accidents. The issue of responsibility in a risky situation is a notoriously difficult one. Moreover, we know (also from some of the results in Chapter 2) that the attitudes towards risk are different for males and females.

Gaertner and Schwettmann (2007) 'tested' the responsibility issue in another situation that we do not want to present in full detail. In this case, financial aid to Sub-Saharan Africa was considered as an alternative to environmental programmes in the home country. It was stated that starvation either resulted – variant 1 – from a long-lasting drought or – variant 2 – harvests were severely damaged by failures to cultivate self-bred grain. Note that compared to the two variants in the first situation, this African situation aimed at incorporating responsibility aspects not at a personal or *ad personam* level but on an 'impersonal' broader scale. They found that the two quite different reasons for starvation had no influence on the evaluation of their respondents. For example, the frequencies for choosing the sequence 0000 in both variants and the frequencies for picking 1111 in both variants were in each case astonishingly close to each other. Also, the percentages of a switch were more or less the same in both variants. What does this mean? It is possible that, in the African situation, responsibility has to be seen as responsibility taken by a larger entity, i.e. that individual responsibility is absent. The individual African peasant is just a 'small' member of the community who is more or less unable to take an independent decision, for or against self-bred grain. Moreover, we again are confronted here with the issue of risk. Given that large-scale droughts hit certain parts of Africa every other year, should one not seize every opportunity to get out of this dilemma, even at the price of a

---

[1] There is another possibly confounding issue in that the timing of the handicap may also matter. Respondents may have judged that a handicap from birth leads to less suffering than a handicap incurred as an adult. This effect is independent of the responsibility issue, and would go in the opposite direction.

possible failure? It is very possible to argue that taking risks is an ethically acceptable (or even desirable) thing to do in the African situation. If that is the judgment of the respondents, they do not have any reason to 'punish' the unlucky inhabitants of Sub-Saharan Africa.

The work of Gaertner and Schwettmann (2007) introduces the question of responsibility into the traditional Rawlsian framework and more specifically into the debate about the equity axiom. In fact, the issue of needs and handicaps was also one of the starting points for the new theories on 'responsibility-sensitive egalitarianism'.

The theoretical literature on 'responsibility-sensitive egalitarianism' (including equality of opportunity) is rapidly growing. The basic starting point of this literature is the distinction between characteristics for which individuals are to be held responsible and those for which they should be compensated. Of course, the first question then becomes where to draw the dividing line between responsibility and compensation variables. As we have seen, Konow took a very specific stance and focused on the degree of control. Yet, the philosophical debate is less conclusive. As we mentioned in Chapter 2, some authors (Roemer, 1993) have even taken a relativistic position and have suggested that the dividing line between responsibility and compensation could be culture-dependent. The idea of control and of voluntary choice was mainly advocated by Arneson (1989) and Cohen (1989, 1990). They reacted against the original proposal in Dworkin's (1981a, 1981b) seminal articles which was to hold people responsible for their preferences (whether these are controlled or not) but not for their (also innate) resources. More recent defenders of the latter (preferences) view, one of the most influential being Fleurbaey (2008), argue that a focus on control leaves us on a slippery slope where we have to answer metaphysical questions on freedom versus determinism. Moreover, they note that the behavioural model of economics (maximize a given utility function under a set of given constraints) leaves no room for real control.

Within the formal models of responsibility-sensitive egalitarianism the so-called 'responsibility cut' can be located anywhere.

The literature has defined general features which hold for all possible definitions of responsibility and compensation variables. Bossert and Fleurbaey (1996) and Fleurbaey (1995) proposed two basic concepts.[2] We formulate them within the context of income (re)distribution and borrow the informal formulations of Schokkaert and Devooght (2003). The first axiom captures the idea of compensation and reflects an egalitarian perspective. Schokkaert and Devooght call it 'full compensation': 'If two persons are identical on all characteristics for which they can be held responsible, i.e. if they only differ with respect to characteristics for which they must be compensated – then the redistribution mechanism must assign these two persons the same post-tax income' (2003, p. 210). The second notion focuses on the idea of responsibility and indicates boundaries to be imposed on egalitarianism. The authors call it 'strict compensation': 'If two persons have identical compensation characteristics, the differences in their pretax income will only reflect differences in their responsibility characteristics, and hence there is no reason why these differences should diminish through the redistribution process' (2003, p. 210). In the context of income redistribution the second criterion advocates equal taxes (or subsidies) for individuals with identical compensation characteristics. The two criteria look perfectly reasonable and seem both necessary for an adequate responsibility-sensitive egalitarian solution. Yet, one of the most basic insights in the literature is that they are conflicting. It is impossible to satisfy them both, as soon as the marginal effect of the compensation characteristics depends on the level of the responsibility variables (and vice versa).

All this suggests that there are two important questions to be answered. First, where to locate the responsibility cut? Second, how popular are the basic axioms of full and strict compensation? And what if there is a conflict between the two? Schokkaert and Devooght (2003) studied these issues from an empirical perspective by doing

---

[2] The literature contains by now a large amount of variants of these basic axioms. A fascinating overview of the ramifications of the theory can be found in Fleurbaey (2008).

Table 4.4. *Locating the responsibility cut in the income distribution problem*

	Preferences	Resources
Controlled	Elisabeth chooses to work harder and to take less leisure time (CP)	Elisabeth is more productive because she has chosen to develop better skills in the past (CR)
Involuntary	Elisabeth works harder because she has been brought up in a hard-working family (IP)	Elisabeth is more productive because she has a higher natural intelligence (IR)

questionnaire–experimental investigations with samples of first-year university students in three different countries – Belgium (April 1996), Burkina Faso (May 1996) and Indonesia (August 1997). The international perspective created the opportunity to gain some insights about Roemer's (1993) point on culture-dependency. Schokkaert and Devooght present results for two environments: the first is the one of health care financing, the second is the one of income redistribution. In this chapter we focus on the latter, although we will also present some results from the former. We will return briefly to the case of health care financing in Chapter 5.

To answer the first question, i.e. to see where to draw the line between personal characteristics that stand for 'responsibility' and characteristics which elicit compensation, respondents were confronted with a series of simple two-person situations where the two persons differed in only one characteristic. The students could pick from a list of possible income distributions that particular distribution which they considered as 'just'. They also received information about the related tax-subsidy scheme. As with our previous discussion, four cases were distinguished (see Table 4.4), allowing us to compare the acceptance of the two basic approaches.

A priori one would expect little compensation in case CP (preferences under the person's control) and a large degree of compensation in case IR (resources which are not under the person's control).

The specific formulation for the first (CP) case was as follows:

Q 4.7: Both Elisabeth and Catherine have followed the same education and have the same financial wealth at their disposal. They are employed in a similar job and are equally intelligent. Elisabeth *chooses to work very hard* and to take only little leisure time. Elisabeth receives for her labour an income of 300. Catherine, on the other hand, *prefers to take more leisure time* and to work fewer hours a week than Elisabeth. Catherine receives for her labour an income of 200. The government wants to redistribute the income. Redistribution does not influence the behaviour of the two persons. What would you consider to be a just redistribution? Please place an asterisk * in the box of your choice. In row *L* you can add an own ideal redistribution:

	Elisabeth		Catherine	
	Subsidy (+) or tax (−)	Income after redistribution	Subsidy (+) or tax (−)	Income after redistribution
A	− 300	0	+ 300	500
B	− 250	50	+ 250	450
C	− 200	100	+ 200	400
D	− 150	150	+ 150	350
E	− 100	200	+ 100	300
F	− 50	250	+ 50	250
G	0	300	0	200
H	+ 50	350	− 50	150
I	+ 100	400	− 100	100
J	+ 150	450	− 150	50
K	+ 200	500	− 200	0
L				

The three other variants were identical except for the description of the two persons involved. These parts were reformulated as follows:

Q 4.8: (...) Both Elisabeth and Catherine have followed the same education and have the same financial wealth at their disposal. They are both employed in a similar job and are equally intelligent. Elisabeth has been brought up in a *hard-working family*. From this background Elisabeth chooses to work very hard and to take only little leisure time. Elisabeth receives for her labour an income of 300. Catherine, on the other hand, has been brought up in a family which attaches *less value to labour and effort*. In keeping with her background Catherine prefers to take more leisure time and to work fewer hours a week than Elisabeth. Catherine receives for her labour an income of 200.

Q 4.9: Both Elisabeth and Catherine have the same financial wealth at their disposal. Both are born with the same level of intelligence. They are both employed in a similar job. We know that both persons work equally hard. Through effort and zest in the past, Elisabeth *developed skills and techniques* which give her a higher productivity level in the present. Elisabeth receives for her labour an income of 300. Catherine, on the other hand, *did not perform effort in the past to develop skills and techniques*. She therefore achieves a lower productivity level than Elisabeth. Catherine receives for her labour an income of 200.

Q 4.10: Both Elisabeth and Catherine have the same financial wealth at their disposal. They are both employed in a similar job. We know that both persons work equally hard. An intelligence test has shown that Elisabeth has a higher natural intelligence than Catherine. Due to her *higher level of intelligence*, Elisabeth achieves a higher level of productivity than Catherine. Elisabeth receives for her labour an income of 300. Catherine, on the other hand, achieves a lower level of productivity. Catherine receives for her labour an income of 200.

Table 4.5. *Results in the income case*

	Belgium $n = 84$	Burkina Faso $n = 90$	Indonesia $n = 203$
Income case 1: Effort (CP)			
Full compensation	6.1	7.8	9.4
Overcompensation	1.2	6.6	0.0
No compensation	69.5	30.0	53.3
Counter-compensation	23.2	55.6	37.2
Income case 2: Hard-working family (IP)			
Full compensation	9.8	14.4	12.4
Overcompensation	0.0	1.1	0.0
No compensation	70.7	32.2	57.1
Counter-compensation	19.5	52.3	30.5
Income case 3: Acquired skills (CR)			
Full compensation	4.9	10.0	12.1
Overcompensation	0.0	1.1	0.0
No compensation	59.3	32.2	52.0
Counter-compensation	35.8	56.7	35.9
Income case 4: Innate intelligence (IR)			
Full compensation	59.8	41.1	46.5
Overcompensation	1.2	1.1	1.8
No compensation	34.1	28.9	37.8
Counter-compensation	4.9	28.9	13.9

The results (in terms of percentages) are summarized in a condensed form in Table 4.5. 'Full compensation' means that the respondent views the characteristic as a compensation variable and is in favour of equality of the post-tax incomes (solution F). 'No compensation' refers to the case where the differentiating characteristic is treated as a responsibility variable and the respondent supports the concept of 'strict compensation'. This means that the status quo income distribution is respected and there should be no taxes or subsidies (solution G). 'Overcompensation' covers cases A–E, where the respondent wants to redistribute so much that the less productive Catherine ends up with a larger post-tax income than the more productive Elisabeth. Finally, 'counter-compensation' goes in the opposite direction, i.e. a tax on the least productive individual and a subsidy for the more productive individual, leading to an increase in the income differences from the pre-tax to the post-tax situation.

There are at least two striking findings in Table 4.5. First, the full compensation idea (leading to an equal post-tax income distribution) is *not* very popular. Even in the case of differences in innate intelligence (involuntary resources), only half of the respondents are willing to go for full compensation. This result may be context-dependent, however: in the income distribution case differences in income may be linked by the respondents to differences in effort, even if this is not mentioned explicitly in the formulation of the question. And as is quite clear from case 1, there is only a small minority of respondents that is willing to compensate for income differences reflecting differences in effort. Second, very surprisingly in the light of the theory, large groups of respondents advocate counter-compensation, i.e. a widening of the pre-tax income differences, even in the case of innate intelligence. This idea does not figure in the literature at all. Apparently, these respondents feel that individuals have a duty to produce and should be 'punished' if they do not perform their duty. Or: they believe that the pre-tax distribution, which supposedly reflects market forces, does not sufficiently reward the more productive individuals.

Table 4.6 is a further summary of Table 4.5, focusing on the responsibility cut. It gives the proportion of respondents in the complete sample that want to compensate, i.e. the first two rows of the subtables in Table 4.5. Although the proportion of respondents that

Table 4.6. *Responsibility cut in the income case*

	Preferences	Resources
Controlled	10.2	10.2
Involuntary	12.6	49.7

wants to compensate is very low (as we have seen in Table 4.5) it is still informative to see that respondents want to compensate for resources rather than for preferences (the intuition of Dworkin), and for involuntary characteristics rather than for controlled characteristics (as argued by Arneson and Cohen, and also found by Konow).

At this stage it is useful to bring into the discussion some findings from the health case in Schokkaert and Devooght (2003). In that case two individuals suffer similarly from lung cancer. Health care expenditures are larger for one of the two, however, because (in the four variants respectively) (CP) this individual opts for a private room because this is more comfortable; (CR) his treatment is more expensive because he is a confirmed smoker; (IP) he opts for a private room because he has psychological problems in the presence of other people; (IR) his treatment is more expensive because he has a genetic defect and his natural resistance is weaker. 'Compensation' here refers to a government subsidy to cover part of health care expenditures. 'Full compensation' implies that two persons with the same responsibility characteristics should pay the same personal contribution. 'Strict compensation' implies that two persons with the same compensation characteristics should receive the same subsidy. This means that if medical expenditures differ because of differences in the responsibility characteristics, these differences are to be fully reflected in the individuals' contributions.

Table 4.7 is analogous to Table 4.6. As respondents are much more willing to compensate for health care expenditures than for pre-tax income differences, the proportions in the various cells are higher.

Table 4.7. *Responsibility cut in the health case*

	Preferences	Resources
Controlled	31.8	41.9
Involuntary	73.1	84.8

However, this only strengthens the conclusion drawn from Table 4.6. Both for the preference aspect and for the resource aspect, compensations are larger for 'involuntary' than for 'controlled'. Both for involuntary and controlled, the resource aspect gets more compensation than the preference aspect. All this is quite intuitive. Note, however, that one must qualify carefully the statement that 'respondents are much more willing to compensate for health care expenditures'. This does *not* mean that the full compensation axiom is accepted by the majority of the respondents. On the contrary, it is quite decisively rejected. Even in the case of genetic defects (IR), fewer than 30% of the respondents go for complete equality of personal contributions. Much more common is what the authors call 'intermediate compensation'. This is the case where the person that has to be compensated gets a larger part of the subsidy, but without going so far as to completely equalize the final personal contributions.

To investigate more directly the relevance of the responsibility-sensitive egalitarian framework, and more specifically of the two axioms of full and strict compensation, Schokkaert and Devooght (2003) also formulate questions in which four individuals differ in two dimensions. They work out two variants of that question: one in which the two axioms are compatible, in the sense that there is a solution satisfying both; and another in which it is impossible to reconcile the two axioms. These questions get rather complicated and we will not discuss them in detail. Yet, the results in Table 4.8 are informative as such. Both axioms are only supported by a minority of the respondents. The results in the health case are similar.

Table 4.8. *Acceptance of axioms (income case)*

	Belgium	Burkina Faso	Indonesia
No conflict between strict and full compensation			
Full, strict	29.5	9.1	6.4
Full, not strict	3.3	9.1	1.0
Not full, strict	14.7	30.3	44.7
Not full, not strict	52.5	51.5	47.9
Conflict between strict and full compensation			
Full, strict	–	–	–
Full, not strict	21.3	9.1	2.1
Not full, strict	23.0	36.4	47.9
Not full, not strict	55.7	54.5	50.0

Before concluding, let us note that the intercultural differences are much less pronounced than one might have thought. After all, the respective societies (Belgium, Burkina Faso and Indonesia) are very different. Compensation and intermediate compensation are a bit higher among Belgian students, but not much. Counter-compensation, a somewhat non-liberal attitude, is higher among Burkinese students. In some of the other cases that have not been discussed here, Schokkaert and Devooght found that Indonesian students are more efficiency-oriented and less redistribution-oriented than the respondents from the other nations, but the authors add that these students came from a specific entrepreneurially oriented segment of the Indonesian society.

The different studies in this section suggest that the issue of responsibility is a highly relevant one. All in all, there is some support for the view that individuals are responsible for the preferences with which they identify and also for 'those things' which are under their control. The issue of responsibility in a risky situation is a thorny issue, that would merit further investigation. Moreover, the empirical work has brought up some questions that are perhaps not yet sufficiently tackled by present theories. What to think about the phenomenon of counter-compensation? And would it not be promising to enrich the framework of responsibility-sensitive egalitarianism with a concept of 'intermediate responsibility', that would thus be consistent with the above findings of intermediate rather than full compensation?

4.2 THE CLAIMS PROBLEM AND THE PROPORTIONAL SOLUTION

The question of how to handle acquired rights is essential in many real-world distribution problems. How to cut social benefits if the budget turns out to be too low to keep all promises? How to compensate the creditors of a firm that goes bankrupt? Which form of wage moderation is most acceptable when such moderation is made necessary by economic circumstances? Although the specific economic context is very different in these examples, the formal structure of the problem is the same. It can be described in general terms as follows: how ought an amount of money to be distributed among a group of individuals if these individuals have differing acquired rights, i.e. different prior claims with respect to the money, and the amount available for distribution falls short of the sum of these claims?

There is a large theoretical literature on this problem – referred to as the 'claims problem', the 'bankruptcy problem', or the problem of 'estate division'.[3] The axiomatic structure of the different solution concepts (or rules) is by now well understood. Yet, since no rule satisfies all *a priori* ethically desirable or logically compelling criteria, there are trade-offs and we still face the problem of which rule to choose. As argued in Chapter 2, this is precisely a situation where empirical research may be helpful. In this section we focus on a few recent questionnaire studies that have analysed this issue. Before turning to the questionnaires, however, we first describe the formal structure of the problem and the most prominent rules. At the end of the

---

[3] An overview of this literature can be found in Moulin (2002) and Thomson (2003).

section we briefly discuss the small experimental literature on how people behave when they are confronted with a claims problem in the lab.

We need some formal notation to explain the exact content of the most important solution concepts. Assume that an amount $E \in \mathbb{R}_+$ has to be divided among a set $N = \{1, 2, \ldots, n\}$ of individuals with claims adding up to more than E. Let $c_i \in \mathbb{R}_+$ denote individual i's claim and $c = (c_1, c_2, \ldots, c_n)$ the claims vector. Claims are ordered so that $c_1 \leq c_2 \leq \cdots \leq c_n$. The total claim $\sum_{i \in N} c_i$ is assumed to be positive and is denoted by C. A claims problem is a pair (c, E) with $C \geq E$. The set $\mathbb{C}$ collects all claims problems. A 'rule' recommends for each claims problem a division between the individuals of the amount to divide.[4] We refer to $R_i(c, E)$ as individual i's award, i.e. what she receives. The difference between the claim of the individual and her award, i.e. $c_i - R_i(c, E)$, is said to be individual i's loss. We assume efficiency, i.e. the sum of the awards equals the amount to be divided. Moreover, no individual receives an award smaller than zero or greater than her claim.

The empirical work has mainly focused on the three oldest and most prominent rules, the proportional rule, the constrained equal awards rule and the constrained equal losses rule. As was illustrated in the very first sentences of this book, the proportional rule already played a central role in Aristotle's theory of justice (Young, 1994). The rule makes awards proportional to claims:

> *Proportional rule (P).* For all $(c, E) \in \mathbb{C}$ and all $i \in N$, we have
> $R_i^{prop}(c, E) = (E/C)c_i$.

The constrained equal awards and constrained equal losses rules both implement the idea of equality, be it in very different ways. Both rules were already discussed by Maimonides in the twelfth century (Aumann and Maschler, 1985). The constrained equal awards rule

---

[4] Formally, a rule is a function R that associates with each claims problem $(c, E) \in \mathbb{C}$ a division $R(c, E) = (R_1(c, E), R_2(c, E), \ldots, R_n(c, E)) \in \mathbb{R}_+^n$.

equalizes awards under the constraint that no individual receives an award that exceeds her claim:

> *Constrained equal awards rule (CEA).* For all $(c, E) \in \mathbb{C}$ and all $i \in N$, we have $R_i^{CEA}(c, E) = \min\{c_i, \lambda\}$ where $\lambda \in \mathbb{R}_+$ is a constant amount chosen so as to satisfy efficiency. An awards vector for the constrained equal awards rule typically looks like $(c_1, c_2, \ldots, c_k, \lambda, \lambda, \ldots, \lambda)$.

The constrained equal losses rule equalizes losses under the constraint that no individual receives a negative award:

> *Constrained equal losses rule (CEL).* For all $(c, E) \in \mathbb{C}$ and all $i \in N$, we have $R_i^{CEL}(c, E) = \max\{0, c_i - \lambda\}$ where $\lambda \in \mathbb{R}_+$ is a constant amount chosen so as to satisfy efficiency. An awards vector for the constrained equal losses rule typically looks like $(0, 0, \ldots, 0, c_k - \lambda, c_{k+1} - \lambda, \ldots, c_n - \lambda)$.

Note that the constrained equal awards rule leads to the best possible results for the lowest claimant (with claim c_1), while the constrained equal losses rule is the best possible for the highest claimant (with claim c_n). In addition to these three rules (the 'three musketeers' as they are called by Herrero and Villar, 2001), many other rules have been proposed and axiomatized in the literature (see Thomson, 2003 and the appendix in Bosmans and Schokkaert, 2009). We will not discuss these other rules in this chapter and we turn now immediately to the questionnaire studies.

A first study is the one by Herrero *et al.* (2010). The main contribution of their paper is the comparison of experimental and questionnaire results, but the latter are worth looking at on their own. Herrero *et al.* (2010) formulate a single formal claims problem, but integrate it in different settings. The formulation of their question is as follows:[5]

---

[5] Herrero *et al.* (2010) have a sixth variant which is set in the context of taxation. This variant (which has also been analysed extensively in the theoretical literature)

Q 4.11:

• The first problem

A bank goes bankrupt and a judge has to decide on how the sum of money obtained from its liquidation would best be divided among its creditors. Obviously, as the bank has gone bankrupt, the sum of creditors' claims (i.e. the sum of their deposits) is much higher than the liquidation funds available. The claims and the available liquidation value, are shown in the following table[6]:

Creditor	Claim
1	5
2	46
3	49

The liquidation value is 20.

The judge has three different options available to him with regard to how the liquiditation value should be shared. They are the following three rules:

1. RULE A: Divide the liquidation value equally among the three creditors, on the condition that no one gets more than her original claim. In other words, this rule benefits the agents with the lowest claim.

2. RULE B: Divide the liquidation value proportionately, according to the size of the claims.

3. RULE C: Losses should be divided as equally as possible among the three creditors, subject to the condition that all agents receive a 'non-negative' amount from the liquidation funds. In other words, this rule benefits the agent with the highest claim.

For the problem in hand, the allocations awarded by each of the above rules are as follows:

requires a reinterpretation of what are 'claims' and 'awards'. Therefore we do not discuss it here.

[6] We reversed the order of the claims to remain consistent with the notation in this chapter.

$$A \equiv (5, 7.5, 7.5); \qquad B \equiv (1, 9.2, 9.8); \qquad C \equiv (0, 8.5, 11.5).$$

For instance, Rule B divides the liquidation value in three parts, assigning 1 to Creditor 1, 9.2 to Creditor 2 and 9.8 to Creditor 3.

What would your choice be if you were the judge?

- The second problem

  In the second problem, the claimants are all shareholders of the bank, rather than depositors.

  What would your choice be if you were the judge?

- The third problem

  In the third problem, claimants are all non-governmental organizations (NGOs) sponsored by the bank. Each claimant had signed a contract with the bank, before its bankruptcy, that stated that they would receive a contribution in accordance with their social standing (i.e. the higher their social standing, the higher the contributions they received). Thus, *'Doctors without Frontiers'*, for instance, should receive the highest endowment, *'Save the Children'* the second highest, and *'Friends of Real Betis Balompié'* the least of all. The judge must now decide on the amounts that they should each obtain.

  What sort of distribution would you decide on if you were the judge?

- The fourth problem

  A man dies leaving three debts. Let the liquidation value in the table above be the estate that he leaves and let the claims be the debts contracted with each creditor.

  What sort of distribution would you decide on if you were the judge?

- The fifth problem

  In the fifth problem, a man dies after having promised a certain amount of money to each of his three sons. The value of the bequest, however, is not enough to cover all of his promises. Thus, his sons are now the claimants and their claims are on the promises their father had made to each of them.

  What sort of distribution would you decide on if you were the judge?

Table 4.9. *'Beauty contest' of solutions in the claims problem (Herrero et al., 2010)*

n = 164	CEA	P	CEL
Depositors	0.06	0.89	0.05
Shareholders	0.06	0.68	0.26
NGOs	0.12	0.46	0.42
Estate	0.15	0.75	0.10
Bequests	0.38	0.61	0.01

This question has several features which make it essentially different from most of the questionnaire studies we have met until now in this book. First, it is really one single question, meaning that all respondents were confronted with all the problems. In a certain sense, they were challenged to compare the different situations explicitly. Second, the respondents were steered to choose between only three possible divisions, each corresponding to a theoretical solution concept. Rule A corresponds to the CEA solution, rule B to the proportional solution and rule C to the CEL solution. One can interpret this way of questioning as a kind of 'beauty contest' between the different rules.[7]

Herrero *et al.* (2010) asked Q 4.11 to 164 undergraduate students at the University of Alicante and at the University of Málaga. The results (in proportions) are summarized in Table 4.9. First, it is obvious that the proportional rule is by far the most popular. Second, there are clear differences between the response patterns in the different settings. These differences can be intuitively understood. In the case of the NGOs the claims reflect needs. It is then understandable that a relatively large group of respondents opts for CEL, which is in this case the most profitable for the most needy. The CEA rule is relatively popular in the case of bequests, where many respondents seem to

---

[7] We borrow the term from Gächter and Riedl (2006) who have a similar contest in their paper.

disregard the promises made by the father and opt for the most equal distribution that is possible. These results suggest that the nature of the claims has a strong influence on the acceptance of the various rules.

As we emphasized before, the setting of Herrero *et al.* (2010) was a kind of 'beauty contest' in which the respondents had to choose among a limited set of results, and in which the different rules were explained in some detail. *A priori*, it is not obvious that respondents would make the same choices in a less structured situation where they have more choice options. In their study, Gächter and Riedl (2006) also had a 'beauty contest' with 59 undergraduate students. As in Herrero *et al.* (2010) the contest was won by the proportional rule. In addition, however, they asked another sample of 29 students an open question, in which the rules were not made explicit. The exact formulation is as follows:

Q 4.12: Please imagine the following situation. You and your bargaining partner have to negotiate over the division of a *total budget of 2,490 money units*. *Historically*, the total budget has always been split *according to performance*. The bargaining partner who has shown the better performance has so far received an amount of *1,980 money units* and the bargaining partner with the lower performance has received *510 money units*. Take it for granted that the performance (i.e. who has shown the higher or lower performance) can be objectively determined. It now turns out that the hitherto valid claims cannot be satisfied any more. The new total budget amounts now to 2,050 money units (i.e. is 440 money units lower than the old budget). According to your opinion, what would be a 'fair' new division from the vantage point of a non-involved, *neutral arbitrator*? (Please give *exact amounts* and no intervals! *The amounts have to add up to 2,050 money units*). Your opinion on the division of the arbitrator:

Amount for the bargaining partner with the better performance . . . .

Amount for the bargaining partner with the lower

performance . . . .

2,050

Gächter and Riedl (2006) formulate a variant of Q 4.12, in which the amount to be distributed and the sum of the claims remain the same, but the claims vector (510, 1,980) is replaced by (850, 1,640), i.e. the spread in claims is considerably reduced. This variant was given to 30 students. It offers the opportunity to check whether respondents pick the same structural solution to claims problems with different structural characteristics. Note that they can only be said to follow a rule (as defined before) if they use the same solution concept consistently for all $(c, E) \in \mathbb{C}$.

Given that respondents can freely fill in their preferred division, there is a large number of answers which do not fit perfectly one of the rules. The authors therefore calculate for each respondent the absolute differences of his or her answer from the three solutions (P, CEA and CEL). They then rank the solutions according to the smallest difference of the proposed and the theoretical division. Table 4.10 gives the results (expressed in absolute numbers of respondents). Column (5) in the table (EQUA) shows the performance of the solution that would divide the budget equally over the two partners, while completely disregarding the claims. The first striking result is that this equal division performs poorly. Claims obviously do matter for the evaluation of the situation. This is not really surprising in the light of the studies described in section 4.1. In the Gächter and Riedl story the different claims reflect differences in performance and we have seen that there is a strong tendency for respondents to reward effort. Second, here also the proportional rule performs best. Summed over the two variants it is ranked first by 54% of the respondents. Third, there is a statistically significant difference between the two variants, in that there is a move from CEL to CEA if the claims vector changes from (850, 1,640) to (510, 1,980). Remember that CEA is the best rule for the lowest claimant. Apparently, the respondents opt for a more egalitarian rule if the spread between the claims gets larger.

Table 4.10. *Ranking of solutions in questionnaire study (Gächter and Riedl, 2006)*

	CEL	P	CEA	EQUA
(1)	(2)	(3)	(4)	(5)
Claims vector: (510, 1,980)				
Amount to distribute: 2,050 ($n = 29$)				
1st rank	4	14	7	4
2nd rank	2	11	16	0
3rd rank	18	4	6	1
4th rank	5	0	0	24
Mean rank	**2.8**	**1.7**	**2.0**	**3.6**
Claims vector: (850, 1,640)				
Amount to distribute: 2,050 ($n = 30$)				
1st rank	6	18	4	2
2nd rank	14	9	6	1
3rd rank	5	3	20	2
4th rank	5	0	0	25
Mean rank	**2.3**	**1.5**	**2.5**	**3.7**

It is important to make a methodological point here. The analysis leading to Table 4.10 is at the level of the individual, i.e. the performance of the different rules is calculated first for each respondent separately. An alternative method would be to calculate first the 'average' division (averaged over all the respondents) and then to look at the distance between this average and the theoretical division. Gächter and Riedl (2006) report that this averaging procedure suggests that rule P is superior in the (1,640, 850) variant, while in the (1,980, 510) variant CEA performs best. Although it is obvious that the analysis at the individual level is to be preferred, this can still be seen as corroborating evidence for the third finding in the previous paragraph.

The last questionnaire study we want to discuss is the one by Bosmans and Schokkaert (2009). As in Herrero *et al.* (2010) they formulate claims problems that are structurally equivalent, i.e. with the same claims vector and the same amount to distribute, in different economic environments. However, contrary to Herrero *et al.* and in line with most of the other studies in this book, the two variants are given to different samples of respondents. The first version is one of wage moderation within a firm and runs as follows:

Q 4.13: Persons A, B and C own a firm together. A, B and C contribute to the activities of the firm in different degrees, and for this reason they have agreed that their salaries differ. They receive monthly €1,500, €2,000 and €2,500, respectively. Each of the three persons has also other sources of income. Due to an unexpected deterioration of the economic circumstances, the part of the revenue of the firm that can be used for salaries in a certain month amounts to only €4,500, not enough to compensate the three firm directors. What is in your view the most just distribution of the sum of €4,500 among persons A, B and C?

	Person A	Person B	Person C
a	1,500	1,500	1,500
b	1,250	1,500	1,750
c	1,125	1,500	1,875
d	1,050	1,500	1,950
e	1,000	1,500	2,000

A second version refers to a cut in retirement pensions. It is formulated as follows:

Q 4.14: Persons A, B and C go on retirement. On the basis of the contributions they have paid during their active career, they are entitled to a monthly pension of €1,500, €2,000 and €2,500, respectively. Due to demographic ageing, these pension amounts can no longer be paid. The government only has €4,500 monthly to spend on the pensions of A, B and C. What is in your view the most just distribution of the sum of €4,500 among persons A, B and C? *(Then follows the same table as in Q 4.13).*

Moreover, each respondent gets nine different versions of either Q 4.13 or Q 4.14. Each of these nine claims problems is a combination of one of three possible claims vectors and one of three possible amounts to be divided. The three possible claims vectors (1,500, 2,000, 2,500), (1,000, 2,000, 3,000) and (500, 2,000, 3,500) have the same sum of claims, but differ in terms of inequality. The three possible amounts to be divided are 4,500, 3,000 and 1500. The table with proposed solutions given above is for the version with the claims vector (1,500, 2,000, 2,500) and the amount to be divided being 4,500. As can be checked easily, for these numbers, solution a is chosen by CEA, solution c by P and solution e by CEL. The other divisions in the formulation of the question correspond to what would be proposed by other theoretical rules or look like reasonable 'intermediate' divisions. The same procedure is followed in the eight other cases, but the proposed divisions are of course different. More details can be found in Bosmans and Schokkaert (2009).

This setting with nine different claims problems allows Bosmans and Schokkaert to elaborate on the finding of Gächter and Riedl (2006) that the respondents opt for a more egalitarian rule if the spread between the claims gets larger. To define what is a more egalitarian solution they use the Lorenz dominance relationship. The literature on inequality measurement considers vectors which are proportional to one another as equally unequal. In that common interpretation, the proportional rule is neutral in terms of progressivity. It preserves the inequality in the claims because it makes the awards vector proportional to the claims vector. A rule is called 'egalitarian' if the proposed division is less unequal than the claims vector. Since CEA always selects the least unequal awards vector available for any rule, it is the most egalitarian rule. On the other hand, CEL is the most

Table 4.11. *Acceptance of solutions (Bosmans and Schokkaert, 2009)*

Rule	Consistency		Lowest distance	
	Firm $(n = 276)$	Pensions $(n = 272)$	Firm $(n = 276)$	Pensions $(n = 272)$
CEA	0	0	2	4
Other 'progressive'	0	0	6	19
P	36	19	71	56
Other 'ambiguous'	0	0	18	20
CEL	2	1	4	2

'anti-egalitarian', as it always selects the most unequal awards vector available for any rule. Some of the other rules are in between CEA and P with respect to progressivity (we call them the 'other progressive' rules) or cannot be ranked unambiguously with respect to P (we call them the 'other ambiguous' rules).[8]

The questionnaire was conducted among 276 first-year undergraduate economics and business students of the Catholic University of Leuven, Belgium, in May 2005, and among 272 second-year undergraduate economics and business students of the University of Osnabrück, Germany, in November 2005. None of the students had already been exposed to the theory of claims problems in their study programmes. Since there were no statistically significant differences between the two groups of respondents, we report only results for the pooled sample.

Let us first focus on a comparison of the results for the 'Firm' and the 'Pensions' versions. These are summarized in Table 4.11. The left-hand part of the table gives the percentage of respondents that have

---

[8] More details on the rules involved can be found in Bosmans and Schokkaert (2009). Bosmans and Lauwers (2007) present an elegant and complete formal analysis of the Lorenz relationships between most of the rules that appear in the literature.

followed consistently the same rule for all the nine cases. Only the proportional rule is really popular, but less so in the Pensions version than in the Firm version.

To get a more complete picture, Bosmans and Schokkaert calculate a 'distance' measure, which is a natural generalization to response patterns over several questions and to problems with more than two claimants of the measure used by Gächter and Riedl (2006). Let (c^ℓ, E^ℓ) be the claims problem used in question $\ell = 1, 2, \ldots, 9$ and denote the awards vector chosen by respondent k in question ℓ by $A^k(c^\ell, E^\ell)$. They then define the distance between the set of awards vectors chosen by k and the set of awards vectors for rule R as $\sum_{\ell=1}^{9} \sum_{i=1}^{3} |A_i^k(c^\ell, E^\ell) - R_i(c^\ell, E^\ell)|$, i.e. as the total money amount that respondent k deviates from what is prescribed by rule R. If a respondent chooses consistently according to rule R, then the distance for R is zero. More generally, the lower the distance, the better the performance of the rule in describing the choices of the given respondent. For each individual, they then consider her response behaviour to be 'closest' to a rule if the corresponding distance is smallest.

The right-hand part of Table 4.11 presents, for each rule, the percentages of the respondents for whom the rule is ranked first, i.e. for whom the distance to the given rule is lower than that to each other rule. For both the Firm version and the Pensions version, the proportional rule clearly performs best. Its superiority is again less manifest in the Pensions version. Both CEA and CEL are extremely unpopular and are beaten by some of the intermediate rules.[9] Bosmans and Schokkaert relate this finding to the structural features of the rules.

---

[9] Among the 'other progressive', Piniles' rule is the most popular. If $E \leq C/2$, $R^{PIN}(c, E) = R^{CEA}(\frac{1}{2}c, E)$.

If $E > C/2$, $R^{PIN}(c, E) = \frac{1}{2}c + R^{CEA}(\frac{1}{2}c, E - C/2)$.

The random arrival rule is the most popular among the 'other ambiguous'. It is closely related to the Shapley value. Assume the individuals arrive one by one, each receiving full compensation until the money runs out. We get the outcome recommended by the random arrival rule by averaging the awards vector obtained in this way over all possible orders of arrival.

In many cases, CEL gives some individuals a zero award. This seems to be very much disliked by respondents. On the other hand, even egalitarian respondents seem to dislike the feature of CEA that it does not respect strictly the order in claims, i.e. that it may advocate equal awards for individuals with different claims. In any case, the results in Table 4.11 suggest that one should avoid an exclusive focus on the 'three musketeers'.

As for the differences between the two versions, Table 4.11 shows that egalitarian rules do better in the Pensions version than in the Firm version. This is again intuitively understandable. First, the status of the differences between the claims of the three individuals is different. In the Firm version, these differences are agreed upon by the three firm owners, while in the Pensions version they are explained by contributions in the past of the three pensioners and hence by wage differences during their active career. Therefore, in the Firm version respondents are likely to interpret the differences between claims to be caused more by effort (a responsibility factor) and less by talent (a compensation factor) than in the Pensions version. Second, the two versions of the questionnaire differ with respect to the relation between the claims or awards and the ultimate outcomes relevant to the three individuals. In the Firm version it is specified that the individuals have also other sources of income. In the Pensions version, on the other hand, it is likely that respondents view the pension amounts as very important, perhaps even the only, sources of income of the three individuals. Moreover, whereas in the Firm version awards pertain only to one month's pay, in the Pensions version the decision on payments is implied to be retained for much longer. We know already from many studies described in Chapter 3 that a concern for the poorest individuals in society (here the individual with the lowest pension claim) tends to be very strong in the case of basic needs. The ethical features of the problem, as reflected in the economic environment, turn out to have a decisive influence on the type of division chosen in problems with acquired rights.

Without going into details, we also briefly summarize the findings when comparing the nine different numerical cases. First, the result of Gächter and Riedl (2006) is confirmed and generalized. For both the Firm version and the Pensions version, more egalitarian solutions become more popular as the inequality in the claims vector increases (while the amount to be divided is kept constant). Second, more egalitarian solutions also become more popular as the amount to be divided decreases (while the claims vector is kept constant). This suggests that an overall perspective on inequality plays a role in the evaluation of different solutions. More particularly, the findings of Bosmans and Schokkaert (2009) may reflect a specific concern for the weakest groups, even in the Firm setting where the claims are closely linked to productive contributions and have been agreed upon by the parties concerned.

All in all, it seems fair to state that the results from the three questionnaire studies described in this section converge quite a lot. While the proportional rule is by far the most popular, acceptance of the different rules may be different in different economic environments. The results in this regard can be meaningfully interpreted in a framework with responsibility and compensation variables. This link has until now not yet been explored deeply in the literature. Moreover, the popularity of more progressive rules seems to increase if the distribution problem gets more 'difficult', in that either the amount to be divided decreases or the inequality in the initial claims increases. This finding, which can arguably be related to a concern for the poorest individuals (with the smallest claim), is not captured by the concept of a rule, to be applied for all $(c, E) \in C$. While the formal structure of the claims problem is by now well understood, there seems to be a need to integrate it in a broader framework with richer ethically relevant information.

As we mentioned at the beginning of this chapter, some recent experimental studies have analysed how individuals 'solve' the claims problem in the laboratory, when they are directly involved and can earn real money (Gächter and Riedl, 2005, 2006; Herrero et al., 2010). The most striking results are found by Gächter and Riedl (2005, 2006),

Table 4.12. *Ranking of solutions in actual negotiations (Gächter and Riedl, 2006)*

	CEL	P	CEA	EQUA
(1,980, 510)				
Amount to distribute: 2,050 (n = 22 pairs)				
1st rank	0	2	5	15
2nd rank	1	5	16	1
3rd rank	5	15	1	0
4th rank	16	0	0	6
Mean rank	**3.7**	**2.6**	**1.8**	**1.9**
(1,640, 850)				
Amount to distribute: 2,050 (n = 9 pairs)				
1st rank	0	2	4	3
2nd rank	1	3	4	1
3rd rank	2	4	1	2
4th rank	6	0	0	3
Mean rank	**3.6**	**2.3**	**1.7**	**2.6**

who opt for a design with free-form bargaining. The decision problem was the same as described in Q 4.12. Subjects were paired and participated first in a knowledge quiz to determine which of the two bargainers was the high or the low claimant. Before the bargaining process started they were asked about their own perception of what would be a 'fair' distribution of the salaries from the point of view of a neutral arbitrator. These claims turned out to be very asymmetric, with the proportional division again the most frequently chosen. Subjective claims had a strong effect on different structural features of the bargaining process such as bargaining duration and concession behaviour (Gächter and Riedl, 2005). The final outcomes in the actual negotiations can be related to the various solution concepts in the same way as described already. The results are presented in Table 4.12, which is analogous to Table 4.10.[10] It turns out that the actually negotiated divisions are best approximated by CEA, and this despite the fact that *a priori* the subjective claims followed the proportional rule. Gächter and Riedl (2006) suggest that there are two focal points in the negotiations, one being the proportional division according to subjective claims, the other being the equal distribution which would be the natural solution in a symmetric bargaining game. It is indeed striking that EQUA fares much better than in Table 4.10. The results of the negotiations would then be a compromise between P and EQUA. Note, moreover, that EQUA does relatively better and P does relatively worse in the case where the discrepancy in the claims vector gets larger. This seems to confirm the tendency of opting for more egalitarian solutions if the inequality in the claims vector increases, that was also found in the questionnaire studies.

Much more can be said about the link between the normative judgments derived in questionnaire studies and actual behaviour in a laboratory situation. We will return to these issues in more general terms in Chapter 6. For the moment, it is sufficient to note that subjectively perceived rights ('moral property rights' in the terminology of Gächter and Riedl, 2005) seem to have a significant influence on the course and the outcomes of actual negotiation processes.

4.3 BENEFITS AND HARMS

In previous sections we have encountered many cases where the distributive principle chosen depends on the specific economic context in which the problem was set. In most of these cases, there was an ethically sound and intuitively understandable reason for the context-dependency. The differences between the situations could therefore be seen as 'real' and relevant. However, in some cases choices may depend on the framing of the problem, even if both the situation and the choice options are basically the same in all ethically relevant

---

[10] Nine pairs did not reach an agreement in the negotiation phase. They are not taken up in Table 4.12.

respects. This happens particularly in comparisons between a positive and a negative formulation of identical outcomes.

Tversky and Kahneman (1981) were among the first to point to this so-called 'framing' issue. Their experiment has become famous. Tversky and Kahneman told participants that the US had two options to prepare for the outbreak of a certain disease, which was predicted to take 600 lives. The respondents were asked to choose between them. When formulated in positive terms of saving lives, the two options were: 200 persons will be saved for certain against a one-third chance that 600 persons will be saved and a two-thirds chance that nobody will be saved. When framed in negative terms of having people die, the two options were: 400 people will lose their lives for sure, contrasted with a one-third chance that nobody will die and a two-thirds chance that 600 people will die. In terms of the number of people surviving, the first option in the first framing is equivalent to the first option in the second framing, and the same is true for the respective second options. Yet, when the problem was framed positively, the participants showed a tendency to choose the option of 200 being saved, while they chose the option with a one-third chance that nobody will die and a two-thirds chance that 600 persons will lose their lives, when the problem was formulated in a negative way.

Gamliel and Peer (2006) investigated whether similar phenomena exist in the context of justice evaluations. In a first experiment, they examined selection procedures, viz. accepting/rejecting students who applied to higher education institutions and accepting/rejecting potential personnel which applied to prospective employers. The distributive principle which was tested was the rule of merit (entrance scores and qualifications, respectively, i.e. a combination of an individual's ability and effort). If the respondents did not want to allocate by merit, the alternative was a random draw. The situations were described in a positive way (to accept half of the applicants) or – relative to the very same situation – in a negative way (to reject half of the applicants). The respondents were 380 undergraduate students in various departments. The results showed that allocation by merit was preferred more under positive framing (acceptance) than under negative framing (rejection). The framing effect was statistically significant in the case of selection for higher education; in the case of personnel selection, it was not.

The second experiment examined five rules of distributive justice. The (non-students') sample included 134 participants, 58 males and 75 females (one person did not state her gender) who worked in various organizations. Three situations were considered. They all described a department in a business organization that employed 50 workers. In each situation, the department had to allocate a different resource to 25 of the workers. In the first situation, the department had 25 new computers and 25 old computers that needed to be allocated, where every worker, of course, preferred the new computers. In the second situation, the department decided to send employees to a professional training programme which would eventually lead to a higher salary. Yet only 25 workers could be sent to the training programme. In the third situation, the department's management needed 25 workers to work 2 hours' overtime in order to accomplish additional tasks.

In each situation, there was a positive and a negative framing. The computer situation was described as either delivering goods (new computers) or as delivering bads (old computers). The professional training programme was framed as either granting or witholding a salary increase. The overtime situation was described as either withholding or delivering the burden of overtime hours. As in the 'beauty contests' of section 4.2, the participants were presented with five options specifying the use of a different principle of distributive justice to determine the allocation: random draw, employee needs, the length of time the worker had been employed (tenure), the employee's ability and the employee's effort. The respondents were asked to rate each principle on a 6-point scale, from 1 ('very unjust') to 6 ('very just').

Table 4.13 presents the descriptive statistics of the respondents' ratings of the five distributive principles for each of the three resources. Column (7) gives an indication of the size of the difference between the

Table 4.13. *The framing effect (Gamliel and Peer, 2006)*

Modes of allocations (resource)		Positive		Negative		(n = 66 or 67)
	Principle	Mean	SD	Mean	SD	Mean difference[1]
(1)	(2)	(3)	(4)	(5)	(6)	(7)
Deliver goods versus	Ability	3.54	1.29	3.16	1.27	0.29*
deliver bads	Effort	3.90	1.23	3.67	1.30	0.18
(computers)	Tenure	3.19	1.28	2.75	1.33	0.33*
	Needs	5.51	0.68	5.36	1.01	0.17
	Equality	3.09	1.52	3.40	1.47	−0.21
Deliver goods versus	Ability	3.90	1.18	3.44	1.42	0.35*
withhold goods	Effort	4.72	1.10	4.74	1.06	−0.02
(training programme)	Tenure	3.46	1.25	2.55	1.39	0.65*
	Needs	4.70	1.30	3.84	1.36	0.62*
	Equality	3.07	1.57	3.27	1.51	−0.13
Withhold bads versus	Ability	2.12	0.99	2.00	0.96	0.12
deliver bads (overtime)	Effort	3.60	1.38	2.88	1.51	0.48*
	Tenure	2.93	1.32	2.73	1.23	0.16
	Needs	4.47	1.14	3.70	1.37	0.59*
	Equality	4.42	1.28	4.09	1.50	0.24

[1] Positive frame mean minus negative frame mean divided by total standard deviation units. An asterisk indicates that the difference is significantly different from zero ($p < 0.05$).

mean ranks in the benefit framing and in the harm framing. The figures reveal that the non-egalitarian principles were considered as more just under positive framing (benefits) than under negative framing (harm). There is only one minor and insignificant exception, which is the effect under the effort principle in the case of the training programme. Statistically significant differences between framing conditions are evident for ability and tenure in the computer allocation case, for ability, tenure and need in the training programme, and for effort and need in the case of working overtime. Remember that the end-states were exactly the same in the negative and the positive framing cases. Apparently, the positive framing of an allocation problem leads to a different encoding of the information than the negative framing of an identical situation. Gamliel and Peer formulate the hypothesis that 'positive framing of a resource allocation should lead to a more favorable association, which will lead to a more favorable judgment of the allocation situation and the principles used to accomplish the allocation' (2006, p. 312).

There are two possible interpretations for this result. The first one (apparently favoured by Gamliel and Peer, 2006) is that the framing effect would also occur in the real world. In that case policy-makers could to some extent manipulate public support for different proposals by formulating them in either positive or in negative terms. The public, on the other hand, perhaps should be made aware of this possibility so as to avoid being manipulated. The second interpretation states that the framing effect is only relevant within the questionnaire setting and relates to the formulation of the questions. Since outcomes are exactly the same, the differences would not appear in the real world and are due to the fact that survey respondents are not sufficiently involved and therefore react to easy cues in the formulation. In this second interpretation the challenge is mainly for researchers, who should be aware of the problem and try to avoid it as much as possible. Without further work, the choice between these two interpretations is not easy, however. Moreover, it is possible that they both capture part of the truth.

The problem is further complicated because it can reasonably be argued that the different reactions on harms versus benefits have a real ethical content in some situations. Schokkaert and Overlaet (1989) asked Belgian undergraduate business students the following question:

> **Q 4.15**: John and Peter are glassblowers and set up a business together. John works 5 days a week and Peter only 4. Their work is complementary and they both are absolutely indispensable. John has a net income of 500,000 BEF a year and Peter earns 400,000 BEF.

Table 4.14. *Dividing a profit versus dividing a loss*

Distribution		% respondents	
John	Peter	Surplus ($n = 40$)	Loss ($n = 39$)
90,000	0	0	0
60,000	30,000	2.5	0
50,000	40,000	82.5	41.0
45,000	45,000	15.0	48.7
40,000	50,000	0	10.3
30,000	60,000	0	0
0	90,000	0	0

After a year, they have got a sales revenue of 990,000 BEF, so that after deduction of their wages they have realized a profit of 90,000 BEF. What would you consider to be a just division of this profit?

This is an example of the so-called 'surplus-sharing' problem (Moulin, 1987). In a second variant, the two glassblowers incur a loss rather than a surplus. The formulation is identical, except for the last two sentences which now read:

> **Q 4.16**: (...) After a year they have got a sales revenue of 810,000 BEF, so that after deduction of their wages, they have incurred a loss of 90,000 BEF. What is a just division of this loss?

The results, summarized in Table 4.14, are striking. First, almost all respondents opt for either a proportional or for an equal division of the surplus and the loss. These are also the focal solutions in theory, and the rules proposed by social psychologists. Second, and most important for the present discussion, there is a strong difference between the positive (surplus) and the negative (loss) case. While more than 80% of the respondents choose a proportional division for a surplus, only 40% do so for a loss. About half of the respondents divide a loss equally over the two agents: this choice implies that the resulting distribution of final incomes (455,000/355,000) is no longer proportional to the number of days worked by the agents (5/4). Apparently the different treatment of gains and losses introduces some path-dependence in this problem.

Yet, is this merely a framing artefact? One could also say that the case of Q 4.16 is not a one-step division problem. As it is formulated, the agents first get an income and only after a year do they realize that there is a loss. In a certain sense one can say that they both have acquired rights with respect to their original income levels and that these rights are equally valued for both agents. In fact, the problem of division of the loss is formally similar to the claims problem that we discussed in section 4.2, and the equal division of the loss corresponds to what would be proposed by the CEL rule. If the original incomes are seen as claims or as moral property rights, there is nothing surprising about the result in Table 4.14. In that case, this is much more than mere framing.

The issue of framing or the different treatment of benefits and losses is a difficult one. In some cases, it may mainly reflect the differential use by respondents (or real-world players) of informational cues in a situation where the outcomes are essentially the same. This is a challenge for empirical researchers, who should be very cautious in choosing the formulation of their questions. If framing is also a real-world phenomenon, it raises tricky issues about how to interpret 'justice' and how to present the available information. Moreover, in some cases, the different reactions on gains and losses can be intuitively understood in terms of acquired rights and claims. It is difficult but essential to distinguish between these different interpretations.

4.4 CONCLUSION

New developments in social choice theory have decreased the distance between the formal models and the ethical intuitions of lay respondents. Principles of justice that are vivid in society can now be cast in formal models. The empirical work has shown that the issues of responsibility and accountability, of acquired rights and claims, of the asymmetry between dividing harms and benefits, are highly relevant to understand real-world opinions. At the same time, the empirical work has suggested a series of questions, that should be tackled by the theory. Where to draw the line between responsibility and compensation variables? How to handle the intuition that full compensation in some cases goes 'too far'? Is counter-compensation ethically meaningful? Is it possible to construct a theory that would explain how the solutions chosen in the claims problem vary with the specific economic context? Is it possible to link this to the issue of responsibility? How to formalize the finding that the proportional solution in the claims problem gets less popular if the spread in the claims becomes larger or if the amount to be divided becomes smaller? Are there other attractive rules which strictly respect the order in claims and do not give any individual a zero award? How to distinguish between the different interpretations for the differential treatment of gains and losses? It can be argued that to answer these questions more empirical and theoretical work is needed and, moreover, that they appear to be highly complementary.

5 Fairness in health

We have focused in previous chapters on general questions from social choice theory. We did not discuss the large bulk of applied questionnaire studies, e.g. about attitudes towards taxation or towards social insurance, that are mainly policy-oriented and that are not framed within a social choice context. Of course each individual questionnaire study that we have discussed describes a case taken from one specific policy setting, but the aim was to derive conclusions that went beyond that specific setting. In this chapter we follow a different approach in bringing together questionnaire studies from one policy domain: that of health care and health insurance. Focusing on one domain may be interesting if one accepts that theories of justice should take into account specific features of the economic environment. Indeed, one of the main findings from the questionnaire studies discussed in Chapters 3 and 4 was that lay opinions about justice do depend on the specific context.

Why focus on health? There can be no doubt that the domain of health policy raises some of the most challenging ethical questions that our societies are facing today. More important for our purposes, the health economic literature contains many questionnaire studies that are closely related to the social choice issues that have been discussed in previous chapters. At the same time, however, the health domain, with its decisions about life and death, involves specific ethical considerations that deserve a special treatment.

The main explanation for the appearance of abstract questions in health economic questionnaires is the need to formulate a coherent criterion for steering allocation decisions in the public health care sector. These allocation decisions often involve a form of priority setting, i.e. of deciding which forms of health care to provide (or to reimburse) for which individuals. Formulated negatively, priority setting can also be seen as a form of rationing. Given the reluctance among policy-makers to introduce monetary valuations in this exercise, the main technique used in practice is cost-effectiveness analysis, in which the output of health care interventions is defined in health terms. The first studies mainly relied on life years gained as an output indicator but this obviously is too crude, since health care interventions do not only influence the duration but also the quality of life. To introduce this consideration, use is now made of the concept of quality adjusted life year (QALY): one QALY corresponds to one year in perfect health, and for each period the quality of life can be scored on a 0–1 scale with 0 corresponding to death and 1 corresponding to perfect health. Negative values correspond to a quality of life that is worse than death. The social objective is then usually taken to be the maximization of total health, i.e. the total number of QALYs:

$$\max \sum_i \sum_t Q_{i,t} \tag{5.1}$$

where $Q_{i,t}$ is the quality of life of individual i in period t, and the sums run over all individuals in society. Under the simplifying assumption that quality of life of individual i after an intervention remains constant, eq. (5.1) simplifies to

$$\max \sum_i T_i Q_i \tag{5.2}$$

where Q_i is the future quality of life and T_i is the number of remaining life years of individual i.

It is immediately clear how this objective function relates to the discussion in previous chapters. First, it is non-welfarist. Although there is some ambiguity with respect to the precise interpretation of quality of life Q in eqs. (5.1) and (5.2) (in principle, it could even refer to subjective well-being), the most common interpretation is in terms of health. Health is an essential but not the only dimension of individual welfare. Second, the additive specification of eq. (5.1) implies that a QALY always gets the same weight, notwithstanding differences in the initial health or in other characteristics of the individuals concerned. As an example, nothing in the rule leads to any compensation for the fact that poorer people in general also have a lower life expectancy and a lower health level. The age effect is especially striking. Since the number of life years gained will normally be larger for a young patient than for an elderly patient, the uncompromising application of eq. (5.1) leads to a preferential treatment of the young. It is not surprising that there is a lot of debate on these distributional consequences.

Survey research has played an important role in the academic debate on these issues. There are two important streams in this literature. First, if one wants to make eq. (5.1) operational, it is necessary to measure quality of life Q_i. For this purpose, experimental and rating scale approaches have been proposed and their pros and cons are heavily discussed. Since measuring health-related quality of life is not a social choice issue, we will leave it aside in the rest of the chapter. We will rather focus on the second stream in the literature, which aims at checking the acceptance of the distributional implications of the objective function itself. In traditional social choice, this distinction between 'measuring preferences' and 'investigating social values' is perfectly clear. Somewhat simplifying, the latter refers to the form of the social welfare function and the former to its arguments. It is important to note, however, that this clear distinction is not made in the bulk of the health economic literature, where the ethical choices are often reduced to mere preferences. The following quote from Dolan (1998, p. 49) is typical:

> If a fundamental prescriptive premise of conventional welfare
> economics is accepted, such that public sector decisions should
> reflect the strength of preferences of those who will be affected by
> those decisions, then it becomes an *empirical question whether*

> *society is prepared to trade efficiency and equity against each other*
> in this (or any other) way. In principle, this framework allows us to
> *derive the precise shape of the health-related social welfare*
> *function from responses to very simple questions* [our italics].

In the same vein, Dolan *et al.* (2003) rightly distinguish between individual and social preferences, where the latter encompass distributional issues. Yet, they again strongly suggest that empirical (survey) work on social preferences can give the final answer to the question of how to specify an ethically acceptable social decision criterion and they claim that there is 'general agreement amongst health economists' in this regard. This means that they take an extreme position in the debate sketched in Chapter 2 and in any case go much further than the reflective equilibrium interpretation that we have endorsed there.[1]

Leaving the problem of QALY measurement aside, there is still a considerable number of questionnaire studies in the health economic literature, mostly focusing on different approaches to the rationing (or priority setting) problem. As in previous chapters, we will not attempt to give a comprehensive survey of this literature, but we will focus on some typical papers and describe these in more detail. Our choice of papers is mainly driven by the existence of a clear link with the issues of general interest discussed in previous chapters. This is perhaps least obvious in section 5.1, in which we briefly describe some typical results about weighting for different needs. Section 5.2 discusses studies that have made use of the concept of the veil of ignorance and section 5.3 introduces the issue of responsibility. In section 5.4 we show the importance of framing and of the reference point in this context. Finally, section 5.5 includes an application of the claims problem. Section 5.6 concludes. Although we focus on general questions, specific features of the health setting will regularly enter the picture.

---

[1] See, e.g., Hausman (2000) and Menzel (1999) for some discussion of this issue.

We should mention from the outset an important limitation of our approach. Even more than in other domains, elements of procedural justice play a role in the debate about rationing health care. Empirical work has confirmed that citizens consider it as crucial that they are consulted, or that decision-makers use the best available scientific evidence in a transparent way. Moreover, they seem to value these procedural features on intrinsic grounds, and not only for their potential instrumental value in leading to better consequences (Anand and Wailoo, 2000; Dolan et al., 2007; Wailoo and Anand, 2005). We will not go into this issue here and stick to the consequentialist approach that has also dominated our previous chapters. As a matter of fact, the question of the relationship between procedures and outcomes is a deep and difficult one, with answers ranging from a complete rejection of consequentialism at one extreme to the position that basically all relevant procedural aspects can be integrated into some sort of broadened consequentialism at the other. A treatment of this general question would go far beyond the scope of this book.[2]

5.1 WEIGHTING FOR DIFFERENT NEEDS

A large number of studies has tried to test directly the sum restriction that is embodied in eqs. (5.1)–(5.2). As an illustration, let us briefly summarize an early study probing the views of Swedish politicians (Lindholm et al., 1997; Lindholm and Rosén, 1998). In Lindholm et al. (1997) a postal questionnaire was sent to 631 persons, which comes to about 40% of all Swedish politicians that were members of local committees with particular responsibility for health care. The overall response rate was 71% ($n = 449$), and there were no clear indications of selective response. We focus on one of their two scenarios (the so-called 'prevention scenario'). There were three versions of this scenario, that were divided evenly over the respondents, i.e. each version

---

[2] See, however, Gaertner and Xu (2004, 2009) and Suzumura and Xu (2001).

was answered by one-third of the respondents. The formulation of version A was as follows:

> **Q 5.1**: In a particular Swedish county 250 people die each year of myocardial infarction. Of these 150 are blue-collar workers and 100 white-collar workers, even though these groups are approximately the same size within the country. Thus, blue-collar workers have a 50% higher mortality from myocardial infarction. As in the country as a whole, health is related to social status. Mortality from myocardial infarction is only *one* obvious example of this but the pattern is similar in the case of, for instance, work-related diseases and cancer. Blue-collar workers also have a shorter life expectancy. Assume that you, as a politician, were to give priority to one of two preventive programmes. One is a population-based programme aimed at reducing risk factors for myocardial infarction in the whole population. The other programme is especially designed to reduce the risk of myocardial infarction in the blue-collar group, but it also influences risk factors in the white-collar group. The latter programme is to be organized in cooperation with employers and industrial health services.

The details of both programmes were presented as in Table 5.1. They are summarized together with the data for the two other versions B and C in columns (1)–(5) of Table 5.2. Each respondent had to compare programme 'All' to one of the three versions of the 'Blue-collar worker' programme. In all these three versions, the mortality rates of blue- and white-collar workers are equalized. However, the total number of cases prevented goes down if we move from version A to version C. One can therefore say that the opportunity cost of equality (in terms of lives saved) gradually increases.

The results are shown in column (6) of Table 5.2, in terms of the proportion of respondents that either prefer the 'Blue-collar' programme or are indifferent between that programme and the (health maximization) programme 'All'. First, looking at the results for version A, it is clear that the simple health maximization rule eq. (5.1) is rejected by a

Table 5.1. *Question format in the 'prevention' scenario*

	Programme 'All'	Programme 'Blue-collar worker'
Efficiency	100 fatal cases of myocardial infarction prevented: 60 in the blue-collar group and 40 in the white-collar group	90 fatal cases of myocardial infarction prevented: 70 in the blue-collar group and 20 in the white-collar group
Equity	The blue-collar workers still have 50% higher mortality, but the absolute number of cases is lower in both groups (90 per year and 60 per year)	Mortality is at the same level in both groups (80 per year)
Costs	10,000,000 SEK/year	10,000,000 SEK/year

Table 5.2. *Details of the versions in the 'prevention' scenario and results*

(1)	(2)	Yearly mortality after the programme (number of cases)			
		(3)	(4)	(5)	(6)
Programme	Prevented cases	BCW	WCW	Total	RESULTS
'All'	100	90	60	150	
Blue-collar version *A*	90	80	80	160	58
Blue-collar version *B*	80	85	85	170	47
Blue-collar version *C*	70	90	90	180	42

majority of the respondents. Almost 60% of the subjects opt for the Blue-collar scenario, despite the fact that this leads to a lower number of prevented cases (and, hence, to more deaths). Second, however, the priority for equality is not absolute. The support for the Blue-collar programmes decreases when moving to versions B and C, in which the efficiency cost of this choice increases. Respondents do not offer unconditional support to either equality or health maximization, but they seem to reason in terms of a trade-off, even in matters of life and death.

Similar results have been obtained in many other studies. It is fair to say that there is by now overwhelming evidence that the simple sum rule is generally rejected by the population (for an overview, see Dolan et al., 2005). In general, respondents agree to give priority to the most severely ill, implying some inequality aversion in the social welfare function, although the strength of the effect seems to depend on the precise framing of the questions (Ubel, 1999). Moreover, respondents do take account of the trade-off between equity and efficiency. This is not at all surprising, of course, in the light of the results that have been described in previous chapters.

Given the challenges raised by the problem of priority setting, health economists went further and tried to find the functional form of the social welfare function that fits best the opinions of respondents. They elicited distributional weights for individuals at different levels of illness (e.g. Dolan, 1998, for an Atkinson-type social welfare function or Bleichrodt et al., 2005, for a rank-dependent specification). In some papers the focus has been on sensitive issues such as the treatment of patients at different age levels (Dolan and Tsuchiya, 2005; Tsuchiya et al., 2003; Doctor et al., 2009). Other studies raised questions similar to those of Lindholm et al. (1997) and looked for the social acceptance of a privileged treatment of lower socio-economic groups to compensate for their lower health (see, e.g., Abásolo and Tsuchyia, 2008). An interesting finding in this regard is that the general public seems to show a greater willingness than clinicians (National Health Service staff involved in service delivery) to sacrifice total health for a more equal distribution (Tsuchiya and Dolan, 2007).

We will return to some of the papers from this stream of literature in the following sections, mainly when they touch issues of more general interest. One general remark should already be made here. As soon as one starts introducing other dimensions (such as age or socio-economic status) into the analysis, and tries to derive differential weights for individuals at different age and status levels, the question arises whether it is still acceptable to focus exclusively on health. Should one not base the weights on the overall situation of individuals, i.e. is it not necessary to aggregate over different dimensions of well-being (as argued, e.g., in Fleurbaey and Schokkaert, 2009)? The most popular approach in economics would then be to turn to welfarism, as 'utility' seems to be a natural aggregator over the various dimensions. Yet we have seen in Chapter 3 that questionnaire–experimental studies (such as that of Yaari and Bar-Hillel, 1984) cast much doubt on the social acceptance of welfarism. A direct test of subjective welfarism in the health setting can be found in Anand and Wailoo (2000). Their question is formulated as follows:

> **Q 5.2**: Imagine a situation where there are two patients suffering from a similar condition. The patients are the same sex, age, and both are single. In such a case, do you think it is acceptable to decide which one gets priority based on an assessment of how much pleasure each person gets from living?

They made use of a postal questionnaire, which was sent out to a sample of Leicestershire residents drawn from the electoral register. A usable response rate of 31% ($n = 144$) was achieved. Only 15 of these respondents (10.4%) took a welfarist position, i.e. answered positively on Q 5.2, while 18 respondents (12.5%) answered that they did not know. Although the question is perhaps too simple and too abstract, the support for subjective welfarism seems to be very weak indeed.

5.2 VEIL OF IGNORANCE

While the direct elicitation of distributional weights undoubtedly leads to useful insights for applied work, in this book we are rather interested in approaches that relate to the foundational questions that have been raised within the social choice literature. From this broader perspective, it is a natural question to ask if the specification of the objective function in eq. (5.1) would be supported behind a veil of ignorance (VOI). We have discussed the VOI approach already in Chapter 3, but the health context, in which risk and insurance play an important role, seems a particularly rich testing ground. The sum-rule eq. (5.1) is indeed reminiscent of utilitarianism although, as said before, Q_i is not generally interpreted as an overall utility indicator. We focus on two interesting papers.

Andersson and Lyttkens (1999) use the VOI framework to ana-lyse the issue of trade-offs that we met in section 5.1.[3] They emphasize that for Rawls the veil of ignorance is a 'thick veil', in the sense that no one knows any of the relevant probabilities. They call this a situation of 'genuine uncertainty', that they oppose to a situation of 'risk', with known probabilities.[4] Using the theory of uncertainty aversion (Schmeidler, 1989), they argue that it is more likely that decision-makers will opt for the maximin criterion behind a heavy veil of ignorance than behind a light veil of ignorance. To inves-tigate the differences between these two situations, they have two different versions of their questionnaire, each given to one-half of their sample.

The 225 respondents were recruited among first-semester economics students at Lund University, who were not familiar with the notion of the veil of ignorance. Five of them, to be decided by a lottery, received a compensation of 500 crowns. The experi-ment was performed in five groups of students. Before the question-naire was distributed, respondents were introduced to the concept of the veil of ignorance, with reference to the work of Rawls.

---

[3] An earlier, closely related, study in a veil of ignorance context is Johannesson and Gerdtham (1996). Their overall results are very similar to those of Andersson and Lyttkens (1999), but they do not have the two different risk scenarios.

[4] Compare to the 'risk' and 'ignorance' scenarios in the study of Traub et al. (2005), that we discussed in section 3.4.

The information, that was projected on an overhead projector and read aloud by one of the authors, included as most important statements:

> The philosopher John Rawls has suggested a procedure that enables individuals to rank societies in an impartial way. He suggests that you should consider viewing society from outside, and that you are placed behind a 'veil of ignorance'. This means that you should imagine that you do not know anything about 'who you are' in society. Consequently, you do not know if you are rich or poor, healthy or ill, etc. By forcing such an impartiality upon yourself, you can rank societies without being influenced by your actual position.

After the introduction, the respondents received one of the two paper versions of the questionnaire. The risk version was formulated as follows:

> Q 5.3 (risk): We will ask you to choose between two societies, A and B. Assume that each society consists of two groups of individuals, group 1 and group 2. The groups differ by having different life expectancies. The groups are exactly alike in all other aspects, for example, they have the same income. We also assume that all individuals live each year of their lives in full health, except for the last two years of life when a reduced quality of life occurs (it is reduced in the same way for all individuals).
>
> Assume now that the two societies are organized in different ways, and that this brings about a situation whereby the life expectancies for the two groups of individuals are not the same across the two societies.
>
> Now you shall choose between these societies without knowing the group in society to which you belong. As we explained in the introduction, you should imagine that you have no knowledge about which group you belong to. Assume that chance determines the

group to which you belong, and that you have an equal chance of belonging to either group. Hence you have a 50% probability of belonging to each group.

Which society (A or B) do you choose if the life expectancies for the two groups are distributed according to the table below? Remember what we said about all individuals living all their years – except the two last years – in full health:

	Society A	Society B
Life expectancy in group 1	88	82
Life expectancy in group 2	66	68

There were six different variants of the table with life expectancies, manipulating two dimensions: the starting positions and the trade-off. There were two different 'reference positions' (society A). The one given above (88,66) corresponded to the large relative difference. It was compared to three societies B: (82,68), (82,70) and (82,72). In each of these cases the life expectancy of group 1 decreases by 6 years, the life expectancy of group 2 increases by 2, 4, or 6 years, respectively. The trade-off is therefore 1/3, 2/3, or 1 year for group 2 in exchange for taking 1 year from group 1. The second reference position A, corresponding to a small relative difference, was (82,68), and it was compared to (76,70), (76,72) and (76,74), implying the same variation in the trade-off.

These same six situations were also combined with the second version of the questionnaire, describing a situation of genuine uncertainty with no known probabilities. This version differed from the previous one in the third paragraph, which now reads as follows:

Q 5.4 (genuine uncertainty): (...) Now you shall choose between these societies without knowing the group in society to which you belong. As we explained in the introduction, you should imagine that you have no knowledge about which group you belong to. This means furthermore that you do not know anything about how probable it is that you belong to one group or the other. In order to comprehend this you can, for example, imagine that you do not know anything about how many people there are in the two groups in society – each can be of any size, large or small, and the difference between the number of people in the groups can be of any size. Which society do you choose if (...).

As mentioned already before, the two versions of the questionnaire were distributed to two different groups of respondents. Overall, the 12 variants of the questionnaire were represented in essentially equal proportions. Taken all these variants together, about 71% of the respondents opted for the egalitarian society B. This confirms once more that the simple idea of health maximization is clearly not supported by the respondents. When comparing the results for the two versions, the authors have to reject the hypothesis that more inequality-averse responses would be given in the situation of genuine uncertainty, without any hint about probabilities. The proportion of subjects choosing society B was 69% for the 'genuine uncertainty' version and 73% for the 'risk' version. In this setting at least (and with these specific formulations), the Rawlsian distinction between uncertainty and risk (and the ensuing justification of maximin) is not relevant for the respondents. The results for the six variants can therefore be pooled over the two versions. They are shown in Table 5.3. In

Table 5.3. *Proportion of subjects choosing 'egalitarian' society* B

Trade-off	Relative difference	
	Small	Large
1/3	0.50	0.60
2/3	0.68	0.81
1	0.80	0.89

line with what we have seen before, both the reference point inequality and the size of the trade-off do matter. Individual respondents behind the veil of ignorance are inequality-averse, but take into account the possible trade-off with efficiency.

Let us now turn to a second study using the VOI approach. In Chapter 3 we discussed some evidence suggesting that respondents take a different position behind a veil of ignorance, compared to a situation in which they are put in the shoes of an outside observer. Of course, this issue is highly relevant in the health setting, too, and it has been studied by Pinto-Prades and Abellán-Perpiñán (2005). Their study is set in the context of measuring the variables Q in eq. (5.1). They go beyond the problem of measuring individual health-related quality of life, however. Indeed, in the literature, an intense discussion has taken place around the precise interpretation of the variables Q: do these capture individual or social values? One way to interpret the latter is that the variables Q in the social decision function could correspond to a concave transformation of the individual values, so as to capture some inequality aversion. But, then: how to measure these social values? We mentioned in the introduction to this chapter that health economists tend to believe that both individual and social values should be based on preferences. The VOI then seems to be a natural approach to this problem.

The aim of Pinto-Prades and Abellán-Perpiñán (2005) is to derive the social values attached to different health states, comparing the VOI with two other approaches. Three of the health states that they considered are described to the respondents in the following terms:[5]

> *Health state Q.* The person has symptoms as a result of a health problem; symptoms can include numbness, minor problems with movement, or some difficulty with reading or writing. The symptoms do not interfere with the person's usual activities to any

---

[5] Pinto-Prades and Abellán-Perpiñán consider more than three health states in their paper, but for our purposes three will do. Moreover, they do not restrict themselves to the three measurement approaches on which we focus in our discussion.

appreciable extent, but they may affect the person's enjoyment of aspects of their daily life.

Health state X. As a consequence of their health problem the person is unable to live independently. They will be unable to travel alone or shop without help if they did these things previously; and they will be unable to look after themselves at home for some reason (for example, they may not be able to prepare a meal, do household chores, or look after money). They can attend to their bodily needs (such as washing, going to the toilet and eating) without problems.

Health state Y. As a consequence of their health problem the person needs assistance with some basic activities of daily living or needs help from another person with walking. Basic activities of daily living include attending to bodily needs such as washing, going to the toilet and eating.

Their first approach to measure the value of these health states is the VOI. The formulation of the relevant question (for health state X) goes as follows:

Q. 5.5 (VOI): We are going to ask you to imagine the next situation. Imagine that there are two small societies of 200 people each. They are all like you. Both societies are the same in everything except in the health of the inhabitants. In society A there are 150 people with good health and 50 have a terminal illness that will cause their death in a few days. In society B there are 150 people in good health and 50 with a chronic health state like X. With this information, would you prefer to be one of the current members of society A or one of the current members of society B? If you choose to be one of the current members of society A you can be one of the 150 people with good health or one of the 50 people with the terminal illness. If you choose to be one of the current members of society B you can be one of the 150 people in good health or one of the 50 people that are in health state X.

This question is the first step in an iterative process. The process consists in manipulating the number of persons with a terminal illness in society

A and the number of persons with health state X in society B, until the individual is indifferent between societies A and B. Using eq. (5.1) as a statement of social objectives, normalizing perfect health to have the value 1 and death to have the value 0, one can then derive from these numbers the implied value of health state X for the respondent.

The first alternative to the VOI is the so-called 'person trade-off' (PTO) approach (Nord, 1995), one of the most popular approaches to generating social preferences in the context of eq. (5.1). This approach does not question the additive structure of eq. (5.1) (see, e.g., the critical analysis in Doctor *et al.*, 2009), but allows for a trade-off between the numbers of individuals treated and the severity of their disease. It is a typical *'ex post'* approach, in which the respondent is put in the position of a decision-maker who has to take allocation decisions in front of the veil of ignorance. Pinto-Prades and Abellán-Perpiñán (2005) formulate this scenario as follows:

> **Q 5.6 (PTO):** Now we are going to ask you to assume that you are the head of a hospital and you have received an increase in your budget. You can decide to spend this money in two alternative programmes A and B, which will benefit people of your age. Programme A is a new treatment that will totally cure people that right now are in health state X. Without the programme they will remain in state X for the rest of their lives. Programme B is a new medicine that will totally cure people that right now are about to die. Without the programme they will die. The number of people that you can benefit in the two programmes is different with the same budget. We are going to change the number of potential beneficiaries in both programmes and we are going to ask you to decide if you would spend the money in programme A or B in each case. You do not have the possibility of splitting the budget between both programmes.

Starting from Q 5.6, there is again a similar iterative process to derive the value of the health state from a situation of indifference. A third approach is called the 'double gamble' (DG) approach. This is a purely individualistic approach, in which the individual is asked to choose between two risky lotteries from the perspective of his or her own health situation. In this case, the iterative process works by manipulating the probabilities. The formulation is as follows:

Q 5.7 (DG): When somebody has a stroke it is very important to provide medication as soon as possible to remove the blood clot. Otherwise, there can be permanent injuries in the brain that may create important chronic health problems. However, the best treatment (or, better said, the best dose) is not clear. In general, there are two ways of dealing with this problem. The doctor can give the patient two different doses, namely, high or low. The problem of the high dose is that in some patients it can lead to death. The low dose cannot cause death but in some patients can be ineffective and then the stroke can cause brain damage and patients can have health problems for the rest of their life. The success and failure probabilities can be different for each dose. Now we are going to change the success and failure probabilities for each dose and we would like you to tell us which dose you think would be better for you. Assume that you have a stroke. If you take the high dose and it fails you have a 25% probability of dying, but if it is successful you have a 75% probability of restoring your health status to good health. If you take the low dose and it fails you have a 25% probability of remaining in health state X for the rest of your life, but if it is successful you have a 75% probability of restoring your health status to good health.

The survey was administered to a stratified random sample of 300 respondents, drawn from the general population of the Barcelona area. Given the complexity of the iterative procedure, it was necessary to work with face-to-face interviews, which were conducted by a team of six trained interviewers over a period of two months. In order not to overburden the respondents, the sample was split into two subsamples of equal size, that each completed the different tasks, i.e. the different scenarios, for a subset of health states. The resulting

Table 5.4. *Evaluation of health states in the different scenarios*

Health state	DG	VOI	PTO
Q	0.78	0.76	0.99
X	0.26	0.29	0.77
Y	– 0.04	– 0.15	0.49

measures of the value of health states Q, X and Y are given in Table 5.4.

The results are striking. First, the values obtained in the VOI setting are very close to those obtained from self-interested decisions under risk DG. Second, there is a large difference between the results with VOI and those with PTO. Remember that the state of death gets a value 0. The fact that the implicit values obtained for health states Q, X and Y are larger under PTO means that the outside observer finds it more important to avoid that people die. In fact, this is also confirmed by the very bad health state Y: under VOI this situation is considered to be worse than death (resulting in the negative value in Table 5.4), but this is not true under PTO. One possible explanation for this result is that the so-called 'rule of rescue' was more salient under PTO than in the other situations: this refers to the moral imperative to rescue identifiable individuals facing avoidable death. However, further variants (removing death from the weights calculations) show that this is not a convincing explanation, since the PTO weights remain higher than the VOI ones.

While the setting is completely different, the three scenarios VOI, PTO and DG are strikingly similar to the scenarios VOI, ISO and PIR that were implemented in the study by Bosmans and Schokkaert (2004), as summarized in Chapter 3. The VOI and PTO treatments are also closely related to the two interpretations of the veil of ignorance (involved evaluator versus outside observer) in the paper by Amiel *et al.* (2009). Although caution is needed when comparing the answers on questions with such a very different formulation, it remains true that the results in the two settings are certainly not contradictory. We argued in Chapter 3 that the differences between VOI and PIR probably followed from the fact that externalities and concern for relative position were relevant for the former and not for the latter. If, as seems likely, externalities and concern for relative position play a much smaller role in the health setting than in the income distribution setting, one would expect the differences between DG and VOI to be smaller. This is exactly what is observed in these results. Furthermore, the large differences between PTO and VOI confirm that it is not acceptable to suppose that decisions behind a veil of ignorance would coincide with decisions taken by an ethically motivated outside observer. This important finding seems to be quite robust in a large variety of settings.

5.3 RESPONSIBILITY

Responsibility and accountability crop up in the health economics literature in different forms. The issue of differences in health and in health care needs due to differences in lifestyle is prominent in the real-world debate on rationing and priority setting in public health systems. There is also a lot of questionnaire evidence corroborating the hypothesis that people accept accountability as a legitimate reason for unequal treatment (see, again, Dolan et al., 2005, for an overview of the literature).

A further example is a study by Dolan and Tsuchiya (2009). These authors explicitly introduce inequality aversion and responsibility into the priority setting framework. In the two-person case (and leaving out the time dimension), they propose the following reformulation of the welfare criterion eq. (5.1):

$$W = [\alpha Q_A^{-r} + (1 - \alpha)Q_B^{-r}]^{(-1/r)}. \tag{5.3}$$

Again, the precise interpretation of the variable Q is left open, but it certainly refers to an *individual* measure of quality of life. Inequality aversion is captured in the standard way through the parameter r. Less standard is the introduction of the parameter α. This parameter introduces an asymmetry in the social welfare function, since it reflects the weight given to one group relative to the other. Dolan and Tsuchiya propose to link this asymmetric treatment of different groups to responsibility. Individuals that are largely responsible for their own ill health should get a smaller weight.

They then propose a questionnaire study to estimate both r and α. This study was part of a broader interview. Letters inviting potential respondents were sent out to 1,500 individuals randomly drawn from the electoral register in three wards in York, UK. About one-third agreed to take part, and out of these, 140 respondents were selected based on their background characteristics. The sample of 130 that finally turned up for interview was broadly representative for the population of Yorkshire and Humberside. These individuals got different versions of the questionnaire. We focus on the estimation of the 'asymmetrical weights' α, which are linked to the responsibility issue, and do not go into the results for the inequality aversion parameter r. The part designed to estimate α was answered by 56 respondents.

Dolan and Tsuchiya (2009) argue that α determines the slopes of the social indifference curves at the intersection with the 45° ray from the origin and therefore formulate a choice problem with two groups at the same health level, but with a different level of responsibility. The precise formulation of the question is as follows:

Q 5.8: Imagine that you are asked to choose between two programmes which could benefit two different groups of people. Both programmes cost the same. Without the intervention, patients will die within a few days but with the intervention they will live for another 10 years in good health and then die. People in both groups are 55 years old. They are similar to one another except that those in Programme A have not taken care of their health, whilst those in Programme B have. Please indicate whether you would choose A or B by ticking one box.

Programme (A)	**Programme (B)**
Number of 55 who **haven't** taken care of their health, who will live for 10 more years, rather than die in a few days.	Number of 55 who **have** taken care of their health, who will live for 10 more years, rather than die in a few days.

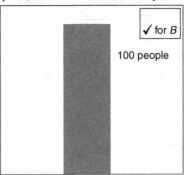

If you chose A, you have now finished. If you chose B, please read on. Choosing Programme B might mean that fewer people can be treated. For each of the four choices below, please tick one box to indicate whether you would still choose B, or whether you now choose A.

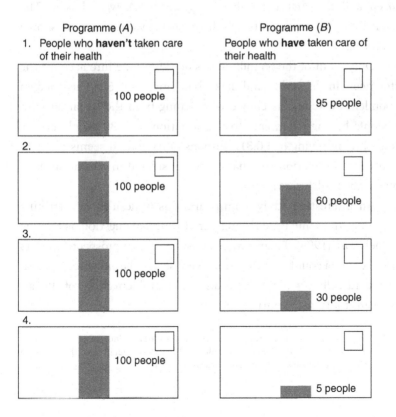

Table 5.5. *Weights and responsibility (Dolan and Tsuchiya, 2009)*

No. of people who have not cared for their health	No. of people who have cared for their health	Distribution of responses $(n = 56)$	Implied α
100	100 or more	1	0.5
100	97.5	4	0.49
100	77.5	21	0.44
100	45.0	24	0.31
100	17.5	1	0.15
100	5 or fewer	5	0.05

The respondent is assumed to be indifferent between the two programmes at the midpoint of the last pair where Programme B was chosen and the first pair where Programme A was chosen. The responses of the respondents and the resulting values for α are shown in Table 5.5.

Only 1 out of the 56 individuals does not take into account the differences in lifestyle (and has therefore $\alpha = 0.5$). The median respondent switches his choice when going from the situation with 60 people having taken care to the situation with 30 people having taken care, implying $\alpha = 0.31$. Responsibility indeed seems to be an essential consideration that has to be considered in allocation decisions in the health care setting.

An interesting study, confirming this basic idea in a striking way, but at the same time raising a tricky ethical question, is the one by Ubel *et al.* (1999). Their sample consisted of 283 prospective jurors in Philadelphia county. These jurors were selected from voter registration records. Ubel *et al.* frame the allocation problem as one of allocating organs for transplantation:[6]

[6] In the fair allocation literature this is a problem of allocating indivisible commodities. Testing carefully the axioms (and solutions) from that literature in the setting of allocation of organs would be a nice research question.

Q 5.9: As you may know, there are not enough hearts available for those who need transplants. This means we need to find some way to decide which people with heart failure should receive transplantable hearts when they become available. We are going to describe some hypothetical situations and ask you to say how you might distribute hearts to people needing transplants. Please answer the questions as if what we describe is the most complete and accurate information available about heart transplantation. Suppose that 200 patients are waiting to receive a heart transplant. They need to receive these transplants within one year or they will die. In that time, only 100 usable hearts will become available.

Ubel *et al.* (1999) distinguished three scenarios to test for the importance of responsibility. In each scenario there was one group of 100 patients without an indication of an unhealthy life, the other groups had a history of, respectively, intravenous drug use, cigarette smoking and eating high-fat diets against a doctor's recommendation. Moreover, there were five versions of the questionnaire for each of these three scenarios. These versions were distributed randomly over the respondents, so that each respondent had to answer only one version. In all these versions, patients not displaying the unhealthy behaviour were described to have a 70% chance of surviving 5 years after transplantation. In three versions, it was claimed that the unhealthy behaviour had caused the illness, but the prognosis was respectively 50%, 70% and 90%.[7] In the two last versions the prognosis was respectively 50% or 90%, but it was explicitly stated that the heart disease had an unknown cause and could therefore not be ascribed to the unhealthy lifestyle. The order of the different versions was randomized, but no order effects were found. The authors therefore look at the pooled results. These are summarized in Table 5.6, in which

---

[7] The better prognosis for those with unhealthy behaviour was 'explained' on medical grounds, e.g. for intravenous drug users it was stated that 'these patients have been shown to do very well after transplant because heroin and cocaine have long term effects on the immune system, making people less likely to reject organ transplants' (Ubel *et al.*, 1999, p. 60).

Table 5.6. *Allocation of available organs (%) (Ubel et al., 1999)*

	% chance of 5-year survival		
Behaviour	90	70	50
Intravenous drug use	33	33	26
Cigarette smoking	45	43	36
High-fat diet	48	47	41

we show the percentage of the available organs that goes to the group with the unhealthy lifestyle.

First, as one would expect, the chance of survival does play a role in the average responses: the number of organs allocated to the group with the unhealthy lifestyle increases if the probability of survival increases. However, in all cases, fewer than half of the organs go to the group with the unhealthy lifestyle, even when their chances of survival are better. The relevance of lifestyle differences is clear. Second, the results differ for the different lifestyles. Intravenous drug users are treated in a particularly harsh way. A possible explanation for this differential treatment is suggested by a third finding. There is no difference between the versions where a link was assumed between the behaviour and the heart illness and those versions where this link was explicitly denied. Respondents allocated fewer organs to those with an unhealthy lifestyle (and particularly to intravenous drug users), even if this behaviour did *not* cause the illness. This attitude goes very much against the ethical starting point that individuals should be held responsible for the 'consequences of their choices', and rather suggests that at least some of the respondents want to 'punish' individuals for their 'socially undesirable' behaviour. Is this an ethically acceptable argument for allocation decisions?

The result from Ubel *et al.* (1999) throws a new light on some of the other questionnaire findings on the importance of responsibility.

Let us return for a while to the paper by Schokkaert and Devooght (2003), that focused on the responsibility cut and on the degree of compensation within the framework of responsibility-sensitive egalitarianism. As we have seen in Chapter 4, they observed in some of their questions an unexpected response pattern that they called 'counter-compensation'. This was strongly present in the income distribution cases, if individuals differed in the level of effort. In the health cases, it appears in one instance, that of smoking behaviour. This question goes as follows:

> **Q 5.10**: Luke and Mark are both suffering from lung cancer. They have the same financial wealth at their disposal and earn the same income. Luke and Mark have to be admitted to a hospital for treatment. We suppose that all treatments are effective. Luke has *never been a smoker*. The costs of his treatment in the hospital are 250. Mark, on the other hand, is a *confirmed smoker*. Due to his smoking behaviour, the effects of lung cancer are more serious than the effects of lung cancer for Luke. The costs of the treatment of Mark are 750. The government has to divide 500 as a financial contribution to the costs of the treatments of the two persons and is willing to divide it completely. What would you consider to be a just division of this amount of money?

The results are summarized in Table 5.7, which can be compared to Table 4.5 in Chapter 4. We noted there that full compensation is exceptional, and that intermediate compensation is more common.

Table 5.7. *Compensation for smokers (Schokkaert and Devooght, 2003)*

	Belgium	Burkina Faso	Indonesia
Full compensation	3.2	2.3	6.1
Intermediate compensation	37.2	34.9	38.5
No compensation	45.7	45.3	39.0
Counter-compensation	13.9	17.5	16.4

In the case of smokers, however, there is in all three countries a majority that does not want to compensate. Here, we want to draw attention to the significant minority in each country that goes for counter-compensation, i.e. that opts for a situation in which the smokers have to pay more out of their own pocket, even if their lung cancer is more serious. This counter-compensation is not present in any of the other health cases that have been described in Chapter 4. It is indeed difficult to justify in the framework of responsibility-sensitive egalitarianism, but it is perfectly consistent with the finding by Ubel *et al.* (1999) that respondents want to punish socially undesirable behaviour. If we take this interpretation seriously, it also forces us to think further about the interpretation of counter-compensation in the case of effort and perhaps even about the attitude of the female respondents towards the paraglider in the study of Gaertner and Schwettmann (2007).

These results confront us with some general questions on the relevance of questionnaire studies for ethical reasoning. How to interpret the fact that a significant group of respondents (in the Ubel *et al.* case even a majority) wants to differentiate health treatment (or, for that matter, income taxation) so as to 'punish' socially undesirable behaviour? Does this 'preference' count as a legitimate social value, or could it still be rejected as the result of further ethical thinking? As was argued in Chapter 2, the 'punishment' position is not necessarily ethically valid only because a majority of respondents accepts it. Yet this immediately raises a question about the relevance of questionnaire studies in general. Apparently, it could be sometimes misleading to interpret the seemingly strong support for the accountability idea as equally strong support for responsibility-sensitive egalitarianism. The answers of the respondents may be influenced by psychological mechanisms with a rather doubtful ethical legitimacy. However, we do not think that this undermines the value of the questionnaire–experimental approach. After all, the problem is discovered precisely through the questionnaire studies. If a similar intuition of 'punishment' perhaps has influenced, unconsciously, some philosophers and economists working on responsibility-sensitivity, the questionnaire results can work as a beneficial warning. In any case, the empirical findings underscore the need for caution and careful interpretation.

5.4 GAINS AND LOSSES, BENEFITS AND HARMS

Allocation decisions in the health context refer to the allocation of health care to different groups of ill patients. In the status quo position, i.e. without additional health care, different individuals are in a different state of illness. Of course, the implicit assumption is that health care will lead to desirable health improvements. Efficiency considerations usually force us to think in marginal terms, i.e. to focus on these gains (and, possibly, losses). A focus on the distribution of gains and losses might also be defensible from an equity point of view. Yet this is *not* the standard social choice approach. In the standard approach, the evaluation of policies is not based on the changes *per se*, but on the resulting allocations of final outcomes. This basically means that one neglects the information about the starting point, i.e. the status quo position, to focus only on the end-results. Applied to the health context, what matters for the standard approach is not the distribution of gains and losses (the 'prospective' health status), but rather overall lifetime health. In subsection 5.4.1, we will see whether respondents accept the standard approach or, on the contrary, evaluate equity in terms of gains and losses. In both approaches, threshold effects may play a role. It might be thought that health gains only matter if they are large enough – or, when we reason in the outcome space, if they lead to final health outcomes that are 'sufficiently' good. The question of threshold effects will be discussed in subsection 5.4.2. Moreover, this whole debate confronts us again with the possibility that equivalent outcomes are evaluated differently depending on whether they are formulated in terms of gains or in terms of losses. The relevance of this framing issue in the context of health is illustrated in subsection 5.4.3.

5.4.1 *Gains, outcomes and monotonicity*

'Gain' and 'outcome' egalitarianism are compared explicitly in a paper by Tsuchiya and Dolan (2009). They argue that the relative popularity of these two views may depend on the perceived unfairness of the status quo position. Suppose that initial health inequalities between socio-economic groups are seen as unacceptable, e.g. because those who are disadvantaged in terms of health are also those who are disadvantaged in terms of economic opportunities. It then seems natural that health policy should aim at rectifying this injustice and should focus on final outcomes. It might even be possible that respondents care so much about the inequality in final outcomes that they reject Pareto-improving changes. Suppose on the other hand that health inequalities in terms of gender are seen as rather unproblematic (either because they result from biological differences, and are therefore not caused by society, or because those who are disadvantaged in terms of health are not those who are disadvantaged in terms of economic opportunities). In this case equity concerns could push in the direction of equalizing gains and/or losses.

To 'test' these hypotheses, Tsuchiya and Dolan (2009) set up a questionnaire study with a non-student sample. Letters of invitation were sent out to 2,000 people on the electoral register in Sheffield, UK. In total 257 people agreed to take part, among which a selection was made to ensure that the sample was broadly representative of the population. At the end 128 persons participated in brief discussion groups of 5–8 people, for which they were paid £15. After this group discussion, they were asked, on an individual basis, to complete a questionnaire.

The part of the questionnaire that is relevant for our purposes consisted of two questions. The first question was set in the context of life expectancy, the second one in the context of long-term limiting illness. For both questions, half of the respondents received a variant where the health differences were between higher and lower social classes, the other half received a variant where the differences were between men and women. In conformity with observed reality, men were the disadvantaged group in terms of life expectancy, women were the disadvantaged group in terms of long-term illness. The specific formulation for the life expectancy/social class scenario was as follows:

Q 5.11: While actual life expectancy varies between individuals, on average, people in social class 1 live to be 78 and in social class 5 they live to be 73. Imagine that you are asked to choose between six programmes that will *increase* average life expectancy.

Social class 1	Social class 5
78 + 0 years = 78 years	73 + 2 years = 75 years

☐

Social class 1	Social class 5
78 + 0 years = 78 years	73 + 3 years = 76 years

☐

Social class 1	Social class 5
78 + 1 years = 79 years	73 + 3 years = 76 years

☐

Social class 1	Social class 5
78 + 2 years = 80 years	73 + 2 years = 75 years

☐

Social class 1	Social class 5
78 + 0 years = 78 years	73 + 3.5 years = 76.5 years

☐

Social class 1	Social class 5
78 + 0 years = 78 years	73 + 4 years = 77 years

☐

The six scenarios were presented in random order. Respondents were first asked to choose their most preferred option, then their second preferred scenario and so on. The outcome of this procedure was a complete individual ranking of all six scenarios in order of preference and without ties. The scenarios for the life expectancy case are summarized in columns (1)–(3) of Table 5.8 and they are represented in part (a) of Figure 5.1. In this figure, the health situation of the two groups is denoted H_I and H_J respectively, and the status quo position is represented by S.

Table 5.8. *Choice options (Tsuchiya and Dolan, 2009)*

	Life expectancy (years)			Long-term illness (%)	
	Group *I*	Group *J*		Group *I*	Group *J*
(1)	(2)	(3)	(4)	(5)	(6)
Status quo	73 years	78 years	Status quo	40%	12%
a	+2	+2	a	-7	-7
b	+3	+1			
c	+4	+0	c	-12	-2
d	+3.5	+0	d	-11	-2
e	+3	+0	e	-10	-2
f	+2	+0	f	-7	-2
			g	-14	-0

The story for long-term illness was similar. In that case the 'status quo' prevalence rates were 40% for the disadvantaged group and 12% for the advantaged group, respectively. The different scenarios in terms of gains and losses are shown in columns (4)–(6) of Table 5.8 and in part (b) of Figure 5.1.

The setup of this questionnaire is rich and the complete individual preference orderings contain a lot of information. We focus on two issues. First, consider the relative rankings of the scenarios a, b and c in the life expectancy case and a, c and g in the illness case. These options are all on the line $\Delta H_I + \Delta H_J = C$, i.e. the total health gain (aggregated over groups I and J) is constant. Outcome egalitarians will have the preference ordering (from the most to the least preferred) (c, b, a), gain egalitarians are characterized by the ordering (a, b, c). In addition those who prefer the middle option (b) prefer a programme targeting the worst-off, while at the same time giving a non-zero gain to the better-off. The distribution of the respondents over these various possibilities is given in Table 5.9. A plurality of the respondents can be classified as outcome egalitarians. A sizable

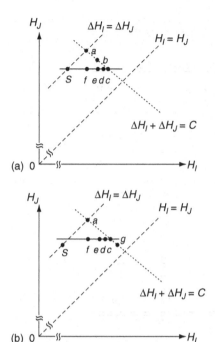

FIGURE 5.1 Graphical representation of choice options (Tsuchiya and Dolan, 2009)

minority, however, is gain egalitarian. Moreover, there is also a significant group preferring the 'middle' option.[8] Note that preferring b over c cannot be rationalized by any social welfare function that is inequality-averse in terms of final outcomes. It is therefore safe to conclude that the distribution of gains as such plays an important role in the evaluations of large groups of respondents. Moreover, a comparison of the scenarios for social class and sex confirms to some extent the hypotheses of the authors: outcome egalitarianism is much more popular in the former than in the latter case. The perceived fairness of the reference point seems to have a large influence on the evaluations.

The relative ranking of a and b with respect to f, e and d on the horizontal line allows the authors to derive conclusions about the curvature of the indifference curves. We will only focus on the aspect of monotonicity. Tsuchiya and Dolan (2009) report that in the life

---

[8] Remember that the same pattern (respondents reluctant to allocate zero amounts) was also found in some of the studies in previous chapters.

Table 5.9. *Gain versus outcome egalitarianism (% of respondents)*

	Social class	Sexes	Total
CASE *A*			
Outcome-based aversion	44	33	38
Gain-based aversion	9	35	24
'Middle' preferred	17	13	15
All others	30	18	24
CASE *B*			
Outcome-based aversion	52	39	45
Gain-based aversion	24	32	29
'Middle' preferred	17	17	17
All others	7	12	10

expectancy case 21% of the respondents prefer *f* over *a* (16% in the social class scenario, 25% in the sex scenario) and 19% of the respondents prefer *e* over *b* (8% for social class, 28% for sex). In the case of long-term illness 28% of the respondents prefer *f* over *a* (26% for social class, 29% for sex). All these choices reveal a rejection of the monotonicity principle. In an earlier study with similar questions on life expectancy in face-to-face interviews, Abásolo and Tsuchiya (2004) even found that more than 50% of a Spanish sample from the general public rejected monotonicity. As we have already seen in Chapter 3, Pareto efficiency is much less cherished by lay respondents than by academic economists. It is striking that this conclusion keeps holding even in matters of life and death.

5.4.2 Threshold effects
It has become clear by now that the simple objective function eq. (5.1) is rejected by a majority of respondents. People do not only care about the total amount of health that is produced, but also about the

distribution of that total amount. The traditional way of capturing this concern is through the introduction of a parameter of inequality aversion, as in eq. (5.3). As noted by Olsen (2000), however, the introduction of such a parameter is not sufficient to represent the distributional preferences of respondents. He notes that a large fraction of Norwegian respondents prefers the option of granting a significant health gain to a few recipients to the alternative option of delivering a small health gain to a larger group. He explains the behaviour of these 'concentrators' by the existence of a threshold effect, i.e. the health gain in the latter option may be deemed too small for the recipients to be able to appreciate it. Yet such a behaviour cannot be represented by a standard inequality-averse social welfare function.

This issue is investigated in a structured way by Rodriguez-Miguez and Pinto-Prades (2002). They conducted a questionnaire-experiment with 61 undergraduate students (21 from economics, 20 from political science, 20 from law). These students were paid approximately $16 for their participation in three meetings. At the first meeting the aim of the study was explained and the respondents filled out a pilot questionnaire to familiarize themselves with the kind of questions asked. The second meeting was the crucial one, in which the respondents had to answer a series of 'person trade-off' (PTO) questions (as described in section 5.2). At the third meeting two weeks later, the experiment was repeated to check the reliability of the answers. The results of this reliability check were reassuring.

In the PTO exercise the respondents had to evaluate five programmes: (1,100), (2,50), (5,20), (20,5) and (50,2), in which the first number refers to the health gain per patient, measured in healthy life years, and the second number refers to the number of patients who would benefit from the programme. For each of these five programmes, the participants had to indicate the number of patients p^* that would make them indifferent between the given programme and the alternative $(10,p^*)$. To help them to answer this question, a so-called 'choice-bracketing' technique was used. The formulation for programme (5,20) was as follows:

Q 5.12: Two treatments A and B differ from each other in the number of additional healthy life years provided to the patient, and in the number of people who receive gains. All patients are 20 years old. You must say whether you prefer treatment A, treatment B, or whether you are indifferent to both of them. Depending on your choice the questionnaire continues in the following way:

If you choose an option where you find the word 'stop', circle the word and go on to the next table (in which treatment A has been varied).

If you choose an option where you find the word 'continue', go on to the next line.

By way of simplification we will use the following notation:

Healthy life year increases for the patient = 'Years'.
Number of people receiving gains = 'People'.
I prefer treatment A = 'Pref. A'.
I am indifferent to A and B = 'Same'.
I prefer treatment B = 'Pref. B'.

The treatments are as follows:

Treatment A		Treatment B				
Years	People	Years	People	Pref. A	Same	Pref. B
5	20	10	1	Continue	Stop	Stop
5	20	10	20	Stop	Stop	Continue
5	20	10	3	Continue	Stop	Stop
5	20	10	18	Stop	Stop	Continue
5	20	10	5	Continue	Stop	Stop
5	20	10	15	Stop	Stop	Continue
5	20	10	8	Continue	Stop	Stop
5	20	10	12	Stop	Stop	Continue
5	20	10	10	Stop	Stop	Stop

Table 5.10. *Average preferences for concentrating and spreading*

(1)	$\bar{p}^*$ (2)	(2,50) (3)	(5,20) (4)	(10,10) (5)	(20,5) (6)	(50,2) (7)
(1,100)	6.74	C*	C**	C**	C**	C*
(2,50)	7.49		C**	C**	C**	S
(5,20)	8.93			C**	C	S**
(10,10)	10				S*	S**
(20,5)	9.23					S**
(50,2)	7.40					

If a respondent is indifferent between two treatments, p^* can be derived immediately. If an interval is the best that can be obtained, p^* is defined to be the intermediate value of that interval. Define $\bar{p}^*$ as the average value of p^* in the sample.

When analysing the answers, it turned out that 16 respondents (26%) did not make any trade-offs: 10 of them always chose the option with the greatest number of patients, 6 of them always the option with the greatest number of years. These lexicographic preferences are not irrational, but they cannot be represented by a continuous social welfare function (SWF). The authors did not include them in their formal analysis. The values of $\bar{p}^*$, calculated for the remaining 45 subjects, are given in column (2) of Table 5.10. Since in all scenarios the total number of healthy life years gained is 100, respondents that are only concerned with this total number should always have $\bar{p}^* = 10$. This hypothesis is strongly rejected.[9] Distribution does matter.

The main objective of the authors is to look for the existence of a threshold effect. To do so, they check whether preferences for concentration of the health benefits and preferences for spreading are both present in the data – and whether these preferences depend on the size

---

[9] The results of the statistical testing procedures can be found in Rodriguez-Miguez and Pinto-Prades (2002).

of the individual health gains. Their hypothesis is that concentrating the health gains on a smaller number of patients might be preferable if the individual health gains otherwise would be so small as to become negligible. They define preferences for concentration and for spreading in a formal way. Let (t', p') and (t'', p'') be two allocations such that the products of the two elements are equal, i.e. $t'p' = t''p''$ (as in the questionnaire). Here t stands for the number of healthy life years gained and is therefore closely related to the number of QALYs. Assume that we know the corresponding $p^{*'}$ and $p^{*''}$ for each individual. By construction, the individual is indifferent between (t', p') and $(10, p^{*'})$ on the one hand and between (t'', p'') and $(10, p^{*''})$ on the other hand. He or she prefers (t', p') to (t'', p'') if $p^{*'} > p^{*''}$. Define $\bar{p}^{*'}$ and $\bar{p}^{*''}$ as the average values of the corresponding p^*. Participants are then defined as having a preference for concentrating (spreading out) health gains if, when $p' > p''$, then $\bar{p}^{*'} < (>) \bar{p}^{*''}$. The results for all pairwise comparisons between scenarios are given in Table 5.10, where the scenarios are ordered on the basis of t. A 'C' stands for a preference for concentration, an 'S' stands for a preference for spreading. Single and double asterisks indicate that the difference between $\bar{p}^{*'}$ and $\bar{p}^{*''}$ is statistically significant at the 0.10 and 0.05 level, respectively. The results look quite coherent. There is an (average) preference for concentrating when t is small, and a preference for spreading when t gets larger.

Remember that a standard SWF with positive inequality aversion cannot represent preferences for concentration. The authors therefore propose a more flexible specification instead of eqs. (5.1) and (5.3):

$$W = \sum_i \alpha_1 e^{-\alpha_2 t_i} t_i^{\alpha_3}. \tag{5.4}$$

If $\alpha_1 = \alpha_3 = 1$ and $\alpha_2 = 0$, we are back in the simple additive framework of eq. (5.1). If $\alpha_1 = 1/\alpha_3$ and $\alpha_2 = 0$, we get a standard inequality-averse SWF. Rodriguez-Miguez and Pinto-Prades (2002) estimate the parameters of eq. (5.4) on the basis of the answers of the 45 respondents that make trade-offs. The results are nicely represented by the

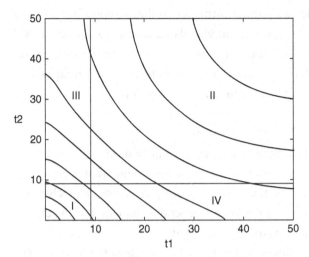

FIGURE 5.2 Preferences and thresholds (Rodriguez-Miguez and Pinto-Prades, 2002)

resulting indifference map, shown in Figure 5.2. The threshold effect (which was already clear in Table 5.10) is confirmed and the threshold is estimated to be 9.1 years. We see standard social indifference curves with a positive inequality aversion, if both t_1 and t_2 are larger than 9.1 (region II). If they are both smaller than 9.1 there is negative inequality aversion with concave indifference curves indicating a preference for concentration (region I). There is no clear pattern in regions III and IV.

This finding of a threshold effect has immediate policy implications. As the authors note (Rodriguez-Miguez and Pinto-Prades, 2002, p. 51), their results may help to explain why programmes that considerably improve the quality and/or the quantity of life of a small number of patients (e.g. organ transplantation), may be preferred to programmes which give very small gains to many patients (e.g. dental fillings). More importantly for our purposes, however, they also relate to more general theoretical issues. In a certain sense, preferences like those depicted in Figure 5.2 bring us back into the discussion on the relevance of a floor constraint (see Chapter 3). It is obvious that the indifference map in Figure 5.2 does not give absolute priority to those below the floor. Yet, the finding of concave indifference curves below the threshold reflects a similar intuition, in that respondents seem to prefer bringing at least some individuals up to the floor, even if as a consequence other individuals below the threshold suffer even more. The subtle relationship between these different interpretations of threshold effects is worthy of further investigation.

5.4.3 A warning: the issue of framing

In all the health questionnaire studies we have discussed until now, the respondents were asked to evaluate allocations that were really different, in terms of either final outcomes or in terms of changes. However, as described in Chapter 4, depending on whether the choice problem is framed in positive or in negative terms, respondents may react differently to different principles, even if the outcomes are identical. Gamliel and Peer (2010) investigated whether this problem was also relevant in the health context. We describe one of their two experiments, which is very similar to the one we discussed in Chapter 4.

Their sample consisted of 210 undergraduate students in Behavioural Sciences (of which 90% were female). These participants were randomly assigned to one of six conditions. For each of three scenarios (heart transplants, lung transplants and AIDS vaccination), there were a positively and a negatively framed formulation. As an example, the heart transplants scenario read as follows:

> **Q 5.13**: In a certain hospital department there are 50 patients suffering from heart disease. All 50 patients' lives are at risk unless they undergo a heart transplant. All other available treatments have been tried and failed. The hospital is expected to receive only 25 hearts for potential transplant patients.

In the positive frame, respondents were then presented with four allocation principles for determining the 25 patients who would receive the resource. They were asked to evaluate the fairness of each of these principles on a 7-point scale (ranging from very unfair to very fair). In the negative frame they were presented with four mirror principles for determining the 25 patients who would *not* receive the resource. The four principles were: (a) merit (patients who are least/ most responsible for their condition would receive/not receive the resource); (b) need (patients who most/least need a transplant would receive/not receive the resource); (c) tenure (patients who had been waiting the longest/shortest time would receive/not receive the resource); and (d) equality (patients who won/lost a random draw would receive/not receive the resource). The two other scenarios (lung transplants and AIDS vaccination) were formulated in a similar manner.

The average evaluations of the principles are given in Table 5.11. It turns out that in all three scenarios the principles of 'merit', 'need' and 'tenure' are more positively valued in the positive framing than in the negative framing variant, and that the differences are statistically significant or nearly significant at the 0.05 level. For the equality principle the differences are minor, go in both directions and are not significant. Gamliel and Peer (2010) interpret these results as a confirmation of their hypothesis that distributive principles in general evoke more positive feelings when the problem is framed in a positive

Table 5.11. *Average evaluations of principles (Gamliel and Peer, 2010)*

Scenario	Framing	Merit	Need	Tenure	Equality
Heart transplants	Positive (n = 30)	3.63	6.23	5.03	4.03
	Negative (n = 30)	2.97	5.50	4.00	3.87
	Difference[1]	0.39	0.53*	0.72*	0.10
Lung transplants	Positive (n = 44)	4.02	5.86	5.48	4.70
	Negative (n = 46)	2.74	4.87	4.33	4.48
	Difference	0.77*	0.71*	0.79*	0.13
AIDS vaccination	Positive (n = 30)	4.30	5.17	3.50	4.43
	Negative (n = 30)	3.23	4.37	2.93	4.87
	Difference	0.55*	0.44*	0.36	−0.23

Note:

1. Positive frame mean minus negative frame mean in standard deviation units. An asterisk indicates that the difference is significantly different from zero ($p < 0.05$).

Table 5.12. *Ranking of principles (Gamliel and Peer, 2010)*

Scenario	Framing	Merit	Need	Tenure	Equality
Heart transplants	Positive $(n = 30)$	4	1	2	3
	Negative $(n = 30)$	4	1	2	3
Lung transplants	Positive $(n = 44)$	4	1	2	3
	Negative $(n = 46)$	4	1	3	2
AIDS vaccination	Positive $(n = 30)$	3	1	4	2
	Negative $(n = 30)$	3	2	4	1

way. They (correctly) note that the 'equality' principle, as they define it, does not fix the final allocation of the transplants, but is rather to be seen as an allocation *procedure*.

There is, however, another way of looking at the same results. Given that all respondents had to evaluate all four principles, it is reasonable to assume that they *compared* the acceptability of these principles, i.e. that they produced relative evaluations. At the average level, these relative rankings can be derived easily from Table 5.11. As Table 5.12 shows, they are remarkably similar and are not strongly influenced by framing. When comparing positive and negative frames, the only differences are the slightly improved position of the equality principle (the case of random allocation) in two of the three scenarios and the lower rank for the needs principle in the negative formulation of the AIDS case. In fact, except in the latter case, the needs principle always comes first. The AIDS case is an exception in still another respect: merit comes always last in the case of transplants, but not in the AIDS vaccination scenario. The 'special' status of AIDS vaccinations (compared to transplants) reminds us of the surprising result of Ubel *et al.* (1999) concerning the treatment of drug users.

The findings of Gamliel and Peer (2010) should be seen as a kind of warning for an uncritical interpretation of the results from questionnaire studies. Framing seems to matter and it should be acknowledged that in this study the final outcomes were really identical and that it is not easy to interpret the differences between the evaluations in terms of 'acquired rights'. On the other hand, the differences in popularity of the various principles in the health setting are smaller than in the firm setting that was described in Chapter 4.

5.5 CLAIMS

The claims problem is a flexible setup that can be used to accommodate many of the intuitions that have been discussed in previous sections. This is even more true if the claims are not exogenously given (as in some of the examples described in Chapter 4), but are rather seen as ethically determined rights. Varying the definition of claims then makes it possible to cover different ethical theories.

The potential relevance of this approach in the health context is illustrated in a questionnaire study by Cuadras-Morató $et\ al.$ (2001). They compare the traditional solutions of the claims problem with health maximization and gain egalitarianism.[10] To avoid confusion, it is useful to define their solution concepts formally. We focus on the two-person case, that was also considered in their questionnaire. Define s_1 and s_2 as the status quo health of the two individuals, i.e. their health status if no additional health resources are allocated. Their health situation after the allocation of the new resources is given by (h_1, h_2). Claims (c_1, c_2) are defined as the legitimate expectations the agents may have about the way resources will be distributed and, as before, we assume that these claims cannot both be satisfied with the available resources, i.e. $(c_1, c_2) \notin P$, where P denotes the set of feasible health allocations. Note that (c_1, c_2) is not defined in terms of resources, but in terms of health.

The first solution is then $health\ maximization$[11]:

---

[10] Cuadras-Morató $et\ al.$ (2001) also analyse (but do not focus on) some solutions from the axiomatic bargaining literature, such as the Nash solution and the Kalai–Smorodinsky solution. We do not discuss these results here.

[11] Cuadras-Morató $et\ al.$ (2001) call this the 'utilitarian' solution, but this terminology is confusing if we reason within a non-welfarist setting.

$$(h_1^{HM}, h_2^{HM}) = \arg\max\{h_1 + h_2 | (h_1, h_2) \in P\}. \tag{5.5}$$

The second one is the *equal increment* solution (h_1^E, h_2^E), that coincides with what Tsuchiya and Dolan (2009) called 'gain egalitarianism', and is characterized by:

$$h_1^E - s_1 = h_2^E - s_2. \tag{5.6}$$

With respect to the solution concepts incorporating claims, Cuadras-Morató *et al.* (2001) do not consider the constrained equal awards solution. Indeed, in their setting, in which nobody can get more than his or her claim by construction, the constrained equal awards solution coincides with the equal increment solution. They take into account the status quo position in defining the two other common solutions to the claims problem. The *proportional* solution is defined in terms of the unsatisfied claims:

$$\frac{h_2^P - s_2}{h_1^P - s_1} = \frac{c_2 - s_2}{c_1 - s_1}. \tag{5.7}$$

The constrained equal loss solution (which they simply call *equal loss*) (h_1^{EL}, h_2^{EL}) aims at an outcome in which the difference between claims and final health states is the same for each patient, i.e.

$$c_2 - h_2^{EL} = c_1 - h_1^{EL}. \tag{5.8}$$

However, no patient should get a negative amount of health improvement. If applying eq. (5.8) leads to an outcome for individual i that is worse than the status quo outcome, the constrained equal loss solution is redefined as

$$h_i^{EL} = s_i \text{ and } h_j^{EL} = h_j^m \tag{5.9}$$

where h_j^m is the health status that individual j can obtain if he gets all of the resources. If the two individuals have equal claims, equal loss tends to equalize the final health states of the patients, and is therefore closely related to outcome egalitarianism.

In their questionnaire study, Cuadras-Morató *et al.* (2001) distinguish two different contexts: one in terms of potential terminal illness (life expectancy), the other in terms of hours of pain (per day). Moreover, they vary what they call the 'capacity to benefit' and the 'health gap'. The former refers to the amount of resources that is needed to reach a given health improvement. Three different levels of relative capacity to benefit are defined: the capacity to benefit of one patient can be twice (five times, ten times) the capacity to benefit of the other patient. The health gap is seen as a measure of relative need and is given by $c_i - s_i$, i.e. the difference between the claim of the individual and her status quo situation. In both contexts, the claims are identical for the two patients. In the 'hours' context, both individuals have a claim of 24 hours without pain. The status quo position is varied between 24, 18, or 12 hours with pain if untreated. The definition of a legitimate claim is more difficult in the 'life expectancy' context. For that context, the authors assume that the claim is a usual life expectancy of 80 years of life. If untreated, patients could die at 20, 40, or 60.

The specific formulation in the 'life expectancy' context was as follows (the italics are ours and indicate where the variations with respect to capacity to benefit and health gap are introduced):

> **Q 5.14**: We are going to show you a simplified problem of decision-making in health care. You have to allocate a certain amount of money between two hypothetical patients. The solution you give to the problem should depend on your preferences, and you should not look for a solution that is objectively the best. We are interested in your opinion about these problems. Thanks a lot for your cooperation.
>
> Assume that there are two patients in a hospital, *A* and *B*. *A* is *20 years* old and *B* is *60 years* old. Each of them has a different illness. Both illnesses are lethal in a short period of time. If *A* and *B*

are not treated, they will die in a few weeks. If they are treated they will reach, at most, 80 years of age (although everybody knows that people die at different ages, we ask you to assume that they will both live in a similar health state until they are 80 and then will die). Each patient has to receive a different treatment. They have to receive treatment for the rest of their lives and if treatment is stopped they will die. Treatment for patient A has an annual cost of *1 million pesetas* and the annual cost for patient B is *0.2 million pesetas*. The budget that the hospital can allocate to both patients is of 20 million pesetas and you have to allocate this money between both patients. We are going to show you several potential ways of dividing the money. We would like you to choose the option that is best in your opinion. A certain amount of money that is allocated to each patient, the corresponding increase in life expectancy, and the corresponding age of death characterize each option.

After this question, the respondents were shown a table with all the relevant characteristics of the different solutions (eqs. (5.5)–(5.9)). They could pick one of these or add another solution of their own. The same procedure was followed for the 'hours of pain' context, for which the introduction was the same as in Q 5.14, but the second paragraph was replaced by:

Q 5.15: Assume that there are two patients in a hospital, A and B. Both suffer from indigestion, which causes them strong headache and sickness. With an appropriate treatment, the indigestion will disappear in 24 hours. In the meantime, we have to give them symptomatic treatment to alleviate the symptoms associated with the indigestion (headache and sickness). Patient A has more severe indigestion, and will have symptoms during the *24 hours* that the indigestion will last. Patient B has less severe indigestion and symptoms will disappear in *12 hours*. The medication to be given to the patients to alleviate these symptoms is different for both patients because of their different physiological characteristics. To eliminate the symptoms for 1 hour, patient A needs medication that costs *10,000 pesetas*. Patient *B* needs medication that costs *5,000 pesetas* to be relieved from symptoms during 1 hour. The hospital can spend 80,000 pesetas to alleviate symptoms of both patients. We will show you different ways of splitting this budget between both patients and you have to choose the option that is the best. These options show the amount of money that each patient will receive, the reduction in the number of hours of pain and discomfort, and the total number of hours without symptoms that each patient will enjoy during the 24 hours that she suffers from indigestion.

Again, the italics (added by us) indicate where the different variations are entered in the description of the case. Taking everything together, the number of potential cases to be analysed becomes 54 (two contexts, three levels of relative capacity to benefit, nine possible combinations of health gaps). The authors surveyed 2,010 students at two Spanish universities (Murcia and Pompeu Fabra at Barcelona), divided into 27 groups. Each subject was given two cases, one from each context, with the other two parameters (capacity to benefit and health gap) different in each case. While the number of students in the groups was different, almost all groups had more than 70 students.

The results for the 'life expectancy' context are given in Table 5.13. Each cell contains the proportion of subjects choosing that solution. We aggregated the different cases in nine groups, according to the relative capacity to benefit of the patients (1–2, 1–5, or 1–10) and according to whether the two patients had the same health gap (equal need), or whether the patient with the largest health gap needed relatively more (more needy less efficient) or less (more needy more efficient) of the resources per life year gained. In some cases the numerical solutions of different approaches coincided: if this happened, the percentages were only calculated for the cases in which it was unambiguously possible to link the respondent's answer to one specific solution concept. This explains why there is one '–' in the table: this is a situation where in all relevant cases the health maximization

Table 5.13. *Results for life expectancy (% respondents)*

		Equal loss	Proportional	Equal gains	Max. health
Equal need	1–2	55			3
	1–5	50			4
	1–10	42			21
More needy	1–2	4	48	35	5
less	1–5	12	30	36	–
efficient	1–10	8	10	43	28
More needy	1–2	30	16	14	1
more	1–5	41	1	7	16
efficient	1–10	32	2	9	12

solution coincided with another rule.[12] In the cases with equal needs, all the claims solutions coincide and we simply took them together in one cell.

The results are interesting. First, in line with all the previous results in this chapter, there is only a minority of respondents opting for health maximization. At the same time, however, this group gets larger if the efficiency cost of more equality increases (i.e. if the relative capacity to benefit goes from 1–2 to 1–10). Second, the claims solutions are relatively popular, and seem to capture well the intuitions of large groups of respondents. However, there is a large variation in their relative success over the various cases. If the more needy is also the more efficient there is not really a conflict between the objectives of egalitarianism and efficiency and the equal loss solution is dominant. Remember that this is close to output egalitarianism. However, if it is relatively more costly to improve the health position of the more needy, the picture is very different. More respondents opt for the

---

[12] Remember that the authors also considered the Nash and the Kalai–Smorodinsky solutions. This also explains why the numbers in each row of Table 5.13 do not add up to 100.

Table 5.14. *Results for hours of pain (% respondents)*

		Equal loss	Proportional	Equal gains	Max. health
Equal need	1–2	81			3
	1–5	66			7
	1–10	64			7
More needy	1–2	49	22	12	2
less	1–5	29	22	21	4
efficient	1–10	17	30	23	8
More needy	1–2	53	7	11	13
more	1–5	33	10	6	17
efficient	1–10	34	1	7	13

proportional solution and for equal gains. As before, efficiency consid-erations do play an important role in the responses. Cuadras-Morató *et al.* (2001) note that an additional explanation is the existence of a 'zero-effect': the equal loss situation is less often chosen if it advocates an allocation in which all the resources go to one individual (the more needy) and nothing to the other. We have already noted the existence of this zero-effect before. The results for the second context (hours of pain) are given in Table 5.14. The setup of this table is identical to that of Table 5.13. The overall pattern of results is rather similar, although there are also some remarkable differences. The equal loss (outcome egalitarian) solution is now much more popular than in the life expectancy context. The proportional solution and, even more clearly, the equal increment solution, are less popular. The same is true for health maximization.

We have already seen in Chapter 4 that the acceptance of differ-ent solutions may be context-dependent. In fact, we argued that there was perhaps need for a 'metatheory', which could rationalize these differences. The study by Cuadras-Morató *et al.* (2001) is an interesting illustration, in that the definition of the claims itself may be subject to discussion. In the hours of pain context, the choice of a painless day as the universal claim for everybody is easy to accept. The situation is different for the claims in the life expectancy context, however. The idea that everybody has a claim to the same number of life years is a specific ethical position (introduced by Williams, 1997, as the 'fair innings' argument), which is hotly debated and far from universally accepted (see also Dolan and Tsuchiya, 2005). In the life expectancy context of Cuadras-Morató *et al.* (2001), it implies a different treatment for people with a life-threatening disease at different ages and, more specifically, a preferential treatment for the young. The equal loss solution will not be attractive for respondents who do not agree with this kind of age discrimination.

In our view, the study by Cuadras-Morató *et al.* (2001) illustrates how many formal and substantial issues related to fair allocation can be cast in the theoretical framework of the claims problem. There is, however, an urgent need for a convincing ethical theory to think about claims, i.e. to define what the ethically legitimate expectations are that people can have in a specific distributive problem.

5.6 CONCLUSION

The health setting is a rich and relevant domain of application for social choice theory. There is general consensus in all studies that distribution matters, i.e. that health maximization as such cannot be an adequate objective for policy. Moreover, many health economists seem to believe that the principle of consumer sovereignty should also hold for drawing conclusions about distributive justice. Although we consider this to be an extreme view, we do of course agree that information about individual distributive attitudes is informative for the ethical debate. In fact, the issues that are raised in the health context are strikingly similar to the issues that come up in the more general social choice context. Health economics could gain from looking more carefully at the social choice literature. Researchers working in empirical social choice can find a wealth of interesting applications and open questions in the health domain.

6 Further observations, views and final remarks

At various instances throughout the book, we promised to come back to certain issues that we consider as fundamental for an understanding and appreciation of the role that empirical social choice can play between the poles of economic theory and political philosophy on the one side and positive (explanatory) social science research on the other. We first reflect on the quality of the information that can be obtained from questionnaire studies. We then discuss the theoretical relevance of the empirical results, especially in the light of the sometimes large degree of intertemporal and intercultural variation in the answers.

6.1 ARE QUESTIONNAIRE STUDIES INFORMATIVE?

Can questionnaire studies provide useful insights at all, if what is being looked at and statistically analysed are, for the most part, the responses of students to relatively simple questionnaires? It might be argued that these responses can be totally arbitrary since any answer could have been given, without any pecuniary consequence for the respondents. Answers could therefore be seen as merely cheap talk – in sharp contrast to most of the laboratory investigations in experimental game theory where money is at stake. Economists usually prefer the latter setup in which participants 'have to put their money where their mouth is'. We have noted already, however, that it is not the aim of 'empirical social choice', as we see it, to predict behaviour. Empirical social choice is interested in eliciting values and individual or societal norms, in particular in relation to the issue of distributive justice, and this is something quite different. We will first argue that there is sufficient evidence supporting the view that the answers to the questionnaire studies are not arbitrary. We will then return to the relationship between questionnaires and experimental games.

6.1.1 Arbitrariness and misunderstandings

Why would respondents express their opinions and sentiments about distributive justice in an arbitrary or even nonsensical way? A presupposition for this kind of answering behaviour was that the students did not take the issues underlying the research programme of the experimenter seriously or that they wanted to ridicule it. Actually, from our own experience, we do not have the slightest clue that this was the case at some point. More importantly, if the answering behaviour of the respondents were arbitrary, this would necessarily have to show in the data. Yet the empirical results are reassuring in this regard.

First, the answers of the respondents are usually very consistent. As an illustration, let us come back to the questionnaire experiments on the Rawlsian equity axiom that were presented in Chapter 3. The issue was, as the reader will remember, either to give a certain amount of money to a handicapped person or to invest the money in the education of intelligent children. The situation for the decision-maker was such that all kinds of answers could have been given over the full sequence, while the number of children to be educated was increasing by 1 from round to round. The reader will probably agree when we say that some of the sequences of possible answering patterns are unintelligible or nonsensical, like (0,1,0,1) or (1,0,1,0), but a quick look back at Table 3.4 with the results for Germany shows that such sequences were not found at all. What pleases us very much is that such strange sequences did not appear in any year over the whole period from 1989 to 2002. There is a somewhat higher frequency of these nonsensical patterns in the results for the Baltics (Table 3.5), but even in this case there is not much reason to worry. In fact, these results may have been due to a lack of understanding.[1] In any case, arbitrariness would yield a different picture.

Actually, in some of the questionnaire studies, simple tests were introduced in order to detect cases of misunderstanding before the

---

[1] The first investigation was run in English, the second, which was done three years later, in the local language. The latter showed fewer 'pathologies'.

respondents were asked to give their evaluation. Jungeilges and Theisen (2011) recently undertook an econometric analysis on the various decision patterns that are possible in the given situation (they expanded their investigation to other situations with the same pattern of decision sequences as in Gaertner, 1992). Their overall verdict is that the results strongly indicate that probands understood the logic of the experiment and responded in a rational manner. More explicitly, the authors state that once a respondent has made a choice (either following the Rawlsian equity axiom or violating it), there is a strong tendency that the person will stick to that decision.

Second, the questionnaire methodology often consists in submitting different variants of the same case to different respondents. These variants usually are differentiated only by a few sentences that suggest an ethically relevant difference in the case description, e.g. by drawing attention to the issue of responsibility. If the respondents were not at all interested and were giving arbitrary answers, one would not expect that these differences in the formulation of the different variants would induce theoretically meaningful differences in the answers. However, the previous chapters contain a wealth of evidence that the differences in the response patterns are meaningful and can be interpreted within a coherent theoretical framework. Actually, they can even contribute to explaining behavioural differences in experimental negotiations about real money amounts (see subsection 6.1.2). Again, arbitrariness would yield a very different picture.

While it seems therefore beyond doubt that ethically *relevant* variations in the descriptions of the cases lead to ethically informative differences in responses, one may suspect that sometimes ethically *irrelevant* variations in the formulation of the questions may also lead to different responses, which in that case could give misleading information about the real ethical opinions of the respondents. This is the issue of framing, that we have discussed already in some depth in earlier chapters. Let us here briefly summarize our position. First, what seems framing at first sight can in fact hide real ethical issues. As an example, it is far from obvious that differences in the status quo position or in the path to arrive at the final solution are ethically irrelevant. Second, if it is impossible to give an ethically relevant interpretation to the response patterns, we should ask the question if the framing effect is only an artefact of the questionnaire environment, or would also occur in the real world. In this latter case, the questionnaire results are still informative. In the former case, extreme care should be taken in choosing the most precise formulation of the question.

A specific issue arises with respect to the comparison of verbal and numerical 'testing' of the same axioms. Previous chapters have shown that the numerical approach strongly dominates in the literature. However, a comparison of numerical and verbal approaches leads to mixed results. Gaertner was worried about this distinction very early on in his own questionnaire experiments and, therefore, presented two different versions of his questionnaires to the students, a so-called 'technical version' that used the social choice tool of extended orderings and a 'verbal version' that circumscribed the technical language. The two versions were, of course, presented to different groups of respondents, but statistical tests did not show any significantly different answering patterns. On the other hand, Schokkaert and Devooght (2003) complemented the analysis summarized in Chapter 4 with a direct testing of the acceptance of verbal versions of the axioms of full and strict compensation. They found that 'full compensation' was much more popular in its verbal formulation than in the numerical results that were summarized in Table 4.8.

In a recent study, Hurley *et al.* (2011) focus explicitly on this methodological issue. Inspired by the Bar-Hillel and Yaari studies (1984 and 1993), they formulate the problem of the distribution of a number of apples between two persons, Jones and Smith. The authors had three versions that they presented to every respondent, viz., a verbal version, a quantitative version and a full-information variant, combining the first two versions. In what follows, we want to concentrate on the first two versions.

In the verbal variant, the authors say that a bag of apples is to be distributed between Jones and Smith. The following information is given which is known also to both Jones and Smith: (a) both persons are identical in all respects except how well their bodies metabolize apples; (b) doctors have determined that Jones's body is better able to derive vitamin F from consuming apples than is Smith's body; (c) both persons are interested in the consumption of apples only insofar as such consumption provides vitamin F. The more vitamin F the better, but the maximum amount of vitamin F that each individual's body can absorb in a single day is 80 milligrammes. Then a few sentences follow that are taken over from Bar-Hillel and Yaari (1993) ('other aspects of the fruit do not matter', etc.). The authors offer five divisions of the bag of apples. We wish to concentrate on two of them: (1) divide the apples in such a way that the total amount of vitamin F obtained by both Jones and Smith together is as large as possible; (2) divide the apples in such a way that Jones and Smith each get the same number of apples.

In the quantitative version, it is said that a bag of 12 apples is to be distributed between Jones and Smith. The following information is given, and is known also to both Jones and Smith: (a) is exactly the same as under the verbal version; (b) doctors have determined that Jones's metabolism is such that his body derives 10 milligrammes of vitamin F from each apple consumed; doctors have also determined that Smith's metabolism is such that his body derives 5 milligrammes of vitamin F from each apple consumed. Then follows (c) as well as some other sentences with exactly the same wording as in the verbal variant. The two ways of dividing the apples we focus on are as follows: (1) Jones: 8 apples (yielding 80 milligrammes of vitamin F); Smith: 4 apples (yielding 20 milligrammes of vitamin F); (2) Jones: 6 apples (yielding 60 milligrammes of vitamin F); Smith: 6 apples (yielding 30 milligrammes of vitamin F).

The authors asked their respondents to pick the 'most fair' and the 'least fair' distribution. We should mention that the winner for 'most fair' was the distribution leading to equal benefits in terms of vitamin F, for both the quantitative and the verbal variant. The reader will remember that this result is perfectly in line with the 'needs' case in Yaari and Bar-Hillel (1984), as discussed in Chapter 3. For 'least fair', the outcome was mixed with respect to quantitative versus verbal, but this is not the point we wish to discuss.

One of the surprises of the Hurley *et al.* (2011) investigation was that under 'most fair', total benefit maximization had 5.6% of the responses in the quantitative variant and 12.1% in the verbal variant. Under 'least fair', total benefit maximization scored 82.4% in the quantitative variant and only 26.9% in the verbal version. Differences are also found with respect to the criterion of equal division of the apples: 15.2% of the respondents selected the equal division of apples as the most fair in the quantitative version against only 7.7% in the verbal variant. The difference was even larger in the least fair variant: 10.5% thought that equal division was least fair in the quantitative version against 45.4% in the verbal version. These are vast differences indeed. How can they be explained or – put differently – what went wrong? Do we face a simple framing effect here, or do we encounter a deeper issue?

What is worrying in the Hurley *et al.* (2011) experiment is that there apparently was a rather profound misunderstanding of basic principles and their consequences. The description 'divide the apples in such a way that the total amount of vitamin F obtained by both Jones and Smith together is as large as possible' sounds persuasive, but in connection with the further information that according to doctors 'Jones's body is better able to derive vitamin F from consuming apples than is Smith's body', the consequence is that there will be a major inequality in terms of numbers of apples allocated to the two persons and in terms of milligrammes of vitamin F consumed. It appears that this mechanism just simply was not understood by several respondents. When the students saw an example with concrete numbers, they decided in large numbers that total benefit maximization was the least fair (82.4% versus 26.9% for the verbal version). The abstract description did not make this clear enough, so it seems. Hurley *et al.* (2011) follow this interpretation. They argue (2011, p. 356) that 'the verbal description of a principle calls for a more deductive style of reasoning, while the actual division calls, if anything, for an induction from a concrete, numeric division back to principles'. This explanation is somewhat less convincing for the differences in the results concerning equal division. The postulate of an equal division can by no means be seen as a highly abstract principle and the partition of a dozen apples into six for each person cannot be viewed either as something particularly demanding as far as arithmetic skills are concerned. Yet, even here, it is possible that some respondents did not realize that an equal division of the apples would not lead to a nearly equal division of the benefits nor, for that matter, to the maximization of total benefits.[2]

How to interpret these findings? That deductive and inductive reasoning do not yield roughly the same inference goes well beyond a mere framing effect, we believe. However, it is not really surprising that untrained respondents do not always see all the relevant consequences of applying principles that are presented to them in a general verbal formulation. After all, a large part of the philosophical and economic literature is precisely about spelling out and evaluating such consequences. The priority given to the numerical approach in most of the empirical work is therefore defensible, as the numerical case descriptions give more and more precise information. Of course, all this also suggests that the responses to the numerical questions will be influenced by the amount of information given and by the way it is presented. Again, there is a clear parallel with the theoretical discussions in which author A will criticize the position of author B, because the latter has neglected some important effects that (according to A) should be incorporated in the evaluation. This issue of what the relevant information is lies at the core of all discussions about distributive justice. It is completely impossible to avoid it. However, it implies that questionnaire results can be highly misleading if one does not take into account carefully the precise formulation of the questions. This is the reason why in this book we have always tried to give all necessary details of the studies.

---

[2] In addition, if the question is formulated in terms of a *ranking* of different principles, differences in the interpretation of one of the principles may change the position of other principles, even if there is no 'confusion' about the latter.

6.1.2 Questionnaires and experimental games

We asserted earlier on that the purpose of the empirical social choice approach is not to forecast actual behaviour in certain competitive or otherwise antagonistic situations where agent 1's gain, let's say, is detrimental to the position of agent 2 or where two or several individuals try to reach some equilibrium position from which neither of them has an incentive to deviate. Actual behaviour can be influenced by a host of aspects, for example by the bargaining talents of the players or their utility from gambling in a staged experiment. While trying to predict behaviour obviously is an essential objective of the social sciences, it is *not* the objective of empirical social choice. The empirical results derived from the questionnaire studies are meant to give information about norms and to act as an input in the normative discussions on distributive justice.

Once we accept this basic distinction between predicting behaviour and deriving information about norms, we can afford to nuance. On the one hand, it would be worrying if there was no link at all between stated norms and actual behaviour. Fortunately, there is by now a growing amount of evidence that the information obtained through questionnaire studies can contribute to a better understanding of decisions where real stakes are involved. In Chapter 4, we discussed the work of Gächter and Riedl (2005, 2006) on the claims problem. They show that answers on questionnaires may give useful information on beliefs and social norms that act as focal points in negotiations about the division of an amount of real money. As another example, Cappelen *et al.* (2011) make their respondents reflect on fairness, in a structured way, before they play a dictator game with production. The results suggest that moral reflection increases the weight people attach to fairness. Moreover, self-reported data on fairness norms have substantial informational value in that, to a great extent, people self-report the fairness ideal that they act upon in the distribution phase. At the same time, however, the self-reports do not add explanatory power to a random utility model estimated on purely behavioural data. Much more work is needed to clarify further the link between norms and actual behaviour and, more specifically, the possible contribution of self-reported data to measuring individual norms. To give but one example, it is not at all surprising that differences are found between bargaining games and dictator games. Yet, it seems fair to conclude that the available experimental evidence supports our position that the answers of the respondents on questionnaires are definitely not arbitrary or nonsensical.

On the other hand, while we believe that people's expressed sentiments are the primary guide in the search for a normative theory (as stated by Bar-Hillel and Yaari in our quotation at the very beginning of this book, p. 3), it would be exaggerated to claim that individual behaviour in an experimental setting is not informative for the ethical debate. As argued by Güth and Kliemt (2010), non-judgmental normative facts like established practices and results of experiments on human behaviour can also be part of the search for a reflective equilibrium. In their view of the world, 'the moral theorist should set out to articulate the normative convictions that might be guiding the justice related actions that are actually observed' (2010, p. 309). Yet a theory of distributive justice is needed in order to identify what are normative convictions and what is mere self-interest in the explanation of behaviour. This is the point where questionnaire studies can make an important contribution.

6.2 FROM EMPIRICAL FINDINGS TO THEORY

When considering the results in previous chapters, one of the most striking findings is the wide diversity in opinions. While we focused most often on the 'dominant' positions, we should not lose sight of the large degree of interindividual variation. Although this variation is not always easy to explain, it shows some structure, e.g. with respect to gender differences. Trying to explain these differences is at the core of the sociological and social psychological work on justice. For our purposes, the interindividual variation obviously raises the methodological issue of who should be the respondents and how to set up the sample for the questionnaire studies. We have already explained our own methodological position in sections 2.2.3 and 2.2.4. Yet, it also raises the deeper question of whether it is meaningful to aim at a universal theory of justice and, more generally, how these varied findings from empirical social choice can contribute to theoretical social choice.

6.2.1 Intertemporal and intercultural variation

The reader will have noticed that most of the studies that we discussed in earlier chapters did not have a time dimension. This may be a bit surprising since one of the major questions which comes to mind when analysing and interpreting results is whether the latter are stable over time or – perhaps – change over time in a systematic way. Actually, the issue of stability or change over time is only one aspect of the broader issue of context-dependence of justice opinions. The context can be the culture, the history of a nation, or the political and social situation.

Let us illustrate this for the example of the trade-off between equity and efficiency. We remind the reader of the early investigations by Yaari and Bar-Hillel where, under the aspect of needs, many respondents were not willing to compensate Smith for the decreasing efficiency of his metabolism endlessly. We concluded in Chapter 3 that the criterion of equalizing the satisfaction of needs at some point collided with the moral intuition of many respondents. A similar phenomenon was witnessed in one of Konow's (2001) investigations where a widening productivity gap between two persons harvesting bananas was honoured more and more by the respondents. Again similar things could be observed in the studies by Cuadras-Morató et al. (2001) within the health context. Health maximization as the guiding principle was not very popular but the group of adherents to this maxim became larger when the efficiency cost of more equality increased. Almost all empirical studies show that respondents are willing to go a long way on the track of equity but they do not do so forever. Where and when the cut occurs apparently depends on various factors.

That broader contextual factors may play an important role in this regard is shown convincingly by the Gaertner *et al.* (2001) investigation in relation to the Rawlsian equity axiom, reported in Chapter 3. First, it is the only real example in empirical social choice of a coherent series of studies over time. It shows that over a longer period the strict adherence to focusing on the worst-off became much weaker while the aspect of longer-term efficiency (expressed by an investment in education) gained momentum. Second, it also shows stunning differences between the German results and the results from the Baltics in 1997–8 and from Vilnius in Lithuania in 2001 (compare Tables 3.4 and 3.5). These differences are so large that in our view they cannot be merely due to differences in wording – cultural, social and political factors must be made responsible for these findings.

The importance of the cultural and political background is not limited to the trade-off between efficiency and equity. We have seen other examples in previous chapters of this book. The reader will remember the results of Amiel *et al.* (2009) on Harsanyi's two models of utilitarianism, the findings of Beckman *et al.* (2002) in relation to the Pareto principle and the results of Schokkaert and Devooght (2003) on the issue of responsibility.

This being so, the question arises whether empirical social choice has shown that the quest for a universal theory of justice is a futile enterprise so that one should better align with Elster's (1992) idea of 'local justice'. If we followed the latter route, we would have to abandon the idea of universality altogether, since there is a multitude of local reasons for proposing certain measures and relinquishing others. According to our view, a more promising path is to look for basic principles (like striving for equity and fairness) that come close to being universally accepted, though universality is contested by specific circumstances such as time and place, culture and history, education and economic prosperity. Abstract economic theory as well as analytical philosophy are – to a very large extent – history-free and culture-independent. However, from a more general perspective, specifying what is truly universal and what can be context-dependent is one of the main challenges for any theory of distributive justice. It is here where empirical social choice may provide additional insights. As a matter of fact, economic theorists and analytical philosophers should also be aware of the potential biases in their own thinking, and empirical results may contribute to this awareness.

6.2.2 Fertilizing the theoretical debate

It will have become clear by now that we see empirical social choice as largely complementary to abstract theorizing. Indeed, the empirical findings in this area are at least partly responsible for the recent trend in social choice theory to abandon the simple welfarist framework. In the present context, we would like to give three examples where findings in empirical social choice can 'fertilize' discussions and debates in philosophy and economics.

The first example refers to the concept of the veil of ignorance which is central in one of Harsanyi's versions of Bayesian utilitarianism and in Rawls' theory. Is the veil of ignorance an attractive construct in the quest for a theory of justice or is the impartial spectator, already widely used in Adam Smith's (1759) *Theory of Moral Sentiments*, a better device in this search? Sen (2009) in his book on *The Idea of Justice*, for example, clearly sides with Smith. Recent findings in empirical social choice have shown that the preferences of a rational individual behind a veil of ignorance do not necessarily coincide with the judgments of an impartial observer. In other words, it is not acceptable to suppose that decisions taken behind a veil coincide with the decisions taken by an ethically motivated outside observer. The theoretical discussion would definitely be enriched if we understood (the reasons for) these differences more accurately.

The second example refers to the phenomenon of counter-compensation which became apparent in the empirical study by Schokkaert and Devooght (2003), discussed in Chapter 4. There is an interesting parallel in the experimental literature on the provision of public goods triggered by Fehr and Gächter (2000), who showed that agents are willing to punish non-cooperative behaviour even if this is costly for the punishing agent. If the phenomenon of punishment in Fehr and Gächter's analysis and the phenomenon of counter-compensation in the study by Schokkaert and Devooght are not adequately taken into consideration, grave mistakes will be made when the behaviour and the reaction of agents within communal decision-making are to be forecast. This provides an interesting link to positive analysis. However, from an ethical perspective one can also ask if (or perhaps when) this preference for punishment is a legitimate social value, or when it should rather be rejected.

The third example refers to the finding that the solutions chosen in the claims problem depend on the specific description of the case, as was clearly illustrated in the results of Bosmans and Schokkaert (2009), Cuadras-Morató et al. (2001) and Herrero et al. (2010). Apparently, the perceived ethical legitimacy of the claims has a strong effect on the choice of rule. If claims can be interpreted as needs (NGOs in Herrero et al., 2010), or as highly deserved (salaries in Bosmans and Schokkaert, 2009), they get a large weight and rules such as 'constrained equal loss' become relatively more popular. If claims get less ethical weight more egalitarian rules come to the fore. This is the case in the bequests variant of Herrero et al. or the pensions version in Bosmans and Schokkaert (2009). These results are an open invitation for theorists to go beyond the description of rules in separation and to move in the direction of a theory that would indicate under which circumstances which rules will (should?) be chosen. The link with the theoretical models of responsibility readily suggests itself.

In all this, it should always be remembered that the answers of the respondents will depend on the way the questions are formulated – and the way the questions are formulated depends on the present state of the theory. A good questionnaire will reflect as much as possible the subtleties of present theoretical modelling. Surprising empirical results may then stimulate further theoretical thinking. In turn, richer theoretical models will create a need for richer questionnaires.

To conclude, in our view, empirical social choice should not be opposed to theoretical thinking – the two are complementary. Analogously, there is also complementarity between questionnaire approaches with self-reported data and behavioural experiments involving real money. Rather than pitching these different approaches artificially against each other in a one-eyed way, the best way forward is to explore their deep complementarities.

References

Abásolo, I. and A. Tsuchiya, 2004. 'Exploring social welfare functions and violation of monotonicity: an example from inequalities in health'. *Journal of Health Economics* **23**: 313–29

2008. 'Understanding preference for egalitarian policies in health: are age and sex determinants?' *Applied Economics* **40**: 2451–61

Adams, J. S., 1965. 'Inequity in social exchange'. *Advances in Experimental Social Psychology*, ed. L. Berkowitz: 267–99. New York: Academic Press

Alesina, A. and G.-M. Angeletos, 2005. 'Fairness and redistribution'. *American Economic Review* **95**: 960–80

Alesina, A. and P. Giuliano, 2011. 'Preferences for redistribution'. *Handbook of Social Economics*, Vol. 1A, [eds.]. Benhabib, A. Bisin and M. Jackson: 93–131. Amsterdam: North-Holland

Alves, W. and P. Rossi, 1978. 'Who should get what? Fairness judgments of the distribution of earnings'. *American Journal of Sociology* **84**: 541–64

Amiel, Y. and F. A. Cowell, 1994. 'Income inequality and social welfare'. *Taxation, Poverty and Income Distribution*, ed. J. Creedy: 193–219. Aldershot: Edward Elgar

1998. 'Distributional orderings and the transfer principle: a re-examination'. *Research on Economic Inequality* **8**: 195–215

1999. *Thinking about Inequality*. Cambridge: Cambridge University Press

Amiel, Y., F. A. Cowell and W. Gaertner, 2008. 'Distributional orderings: an approach with seven flavours'. Distributional Analysis Research Paper. STICERD, LSE, London. Forthcoming in *Theory and Decision*

2009. 'To be or not to be involved: a questionnaire–experimental view on Harsanyi's utilitarian ethics'. *Social Choice and Welfare* **32**: 253–74

Anand, P. and A. Wailoo, 2000. 'Utilities vs rights to publicly provided goods: arguments and evidence from health-care rationing'. *Economica* **67**: 543–77

Andersson, F. and C. Lyttkens, 1999. 'Preferences for equity in health behind a veil of ignorance'. *Health Economics* **8**: 369–78

Aristotle, fourth century BC, 1976. *The Nicomachean Ethics* (translated by J. A. K. Thomson). Harmondsworth: Penguin

Arneson, R., 1989. 'Equality and equal opportunity for welfare'. *Philosophical Studies* **56**: 77–93

Arrow, K. J. 1951, 1963. *Social Choice and Individual Values*. New York: Wiley

Atkinson, A., 1970. 'On the measurement of inequality'. *Journal of Economic Theory* **2**: 244–63

Aumann, R. and M. Maschler, 1985. 'Game theoretic analysis of a bankruptcy problem from the Talmud'. *Journal of Economic Theory* **36**: 195–213

Bar-Hillel, M. and M. Yaari, 1993. 'Judgments of distributive justice'. *Psychological Perspectives on Justice*, eds. B. Mellers and J. Baron: 55–84. Cambridge: Cambridge University Press

Beckman, S., J. Formby, J. Smith and B. Zheng, 2002. 'Envy, malice and Pareto efficiency: an experimental examination'. *Social Choice and Welfare* **19**: 349–67

Bell, J. and E. Schokkaert, 1992. 'Interdisciplinary theory and research on justice'. *Justice: Interdisciplinary Perspectives*, ed. K. Scherer: 237–53. Cambridge: Cambridge University Press

Bernasconi, M., 2002. 'How should income be divided? Questionnaire evidence from the theory of impartial preferences'. *Journal of Economics* Supplement **9**: 163–95

Bleichrodt, H., J. Doctor and E. Stolk, 2005. 'A nonparametric elicitation of the equity-efficiency trade-off in cost-utility analysis'. *Journal of Health Economics* **24**: 655–78

Bosmans, K. and L. Lauwers, 2007. 'Lorenz comparisons of nine rules for the adjudication of conflicting claims'. Katholieke Universiteit Leuven: CES Discussion Paper **07.05**

Bosmans, K. and E. Schokkaert, 2004. 'Social welfare, the veil of ignorance and purely individual risk: an empirical examination'. *Research on Economic Inequality* **11**: 85–114

2009. 'Equality preference in the claims problem: a questionnaire study of cuts in earnings and pensions'. *Social Choice and Welfare* **33**: 533–57

Bossert, W. and M. Fleurbaey, 1996. 'Redistribution and compensation'. *Social Choice and Welfare* **13**: 343–55

Cappelen, A., A. D. Hole, E. Sorensen and B. Tungodden, 2011. 'The importance of moral reflection and self-reported data in a dictator game with production'. *Social Choice and Welfare* **36**: 105–20

Carlsson, F., D. Daruvala and O. Johansson-Stenman, 2005. 'Are people inequality averse or just risk averse?' *Economica* **72**: 375–96

Cohen, G., 1989. 'On the currency of egalitarian justice'. *Ethics* **99**: 906–44

1990. 'Equality of what? On welfare, goods and capabilities'. *Recherches Économiques de Louvain* **56**: 357–82

Cuadras-Morató, X., J.-L. Pinto-Prades and J.-M. Abellán-Perpiñán, 2001. 'Equity considerations in health care: the relevance of claims'. *Health Economics* **10**: 187–205 d'Aspremont, C. and L. Gevers, 1977. 'Equity and the informational basis of collective choice'. *Review of Economic Studies* **44**: 199–209

Deutsch, M., 1983. 'Current social psychological perspectives on justice'. *European Journal of Social Psychology* **13**: 305–19

Doctor, J., J. Miyamoto and H. Bleichrodt, 2009. 'When are person tradeoffs valid?' *Journal of Health Economics* **28**: 1018–27

Dolan, P., 1998. 'The measurement of individual utility and social welfare'. *Journal of Health Economics* **17**: 39–52

Dolan, P., R. Edlin, A. Tsuchiya and A. Wailoo, 2007. 'It ain't what you do, it's the way that you do it: characteristics of procedural justice and their importance in social decision-making'. *Journal of Economic Behavior and Organization* **64**: 157–70

Dolan, P., J. A. Olsen, P. Menzel and J. Richardson, 2003. 'An inquiry into the different perspectives that can be used when eliciting preferences in health'. *Health Economics* **12**: 545–51

Dolan, P., R. Shaw, A. Tsuchiya and A. Williams, 2005. 'QALY maximisation and people's preferences: a methodological review of the literature'. *Health Economics* **14**: 197–208

Dolan, P. and A. Tsuchiya, 2005. 'Health priorities and public preferences: the relative importance of past health experience and future health prospects'. *Journal of Health Economics* **24**: 703–14

2009. 'The social welfare function and individual responsibility: some theoretical issues and empirical evidence'. *Journal of Health Economics* **28**: 210–20

Dworkin, R., 1981a. 'What is equality? Part 1: Equality of welfare'. *Philosophy and Public Affairs* **10**: 185–246

1981b. 'What is equality? Part 2: Equality of resources'. *Philosophy and Public Affairs* **10**: 283–345

Ebert, U., 2009. 'Taking empirical studies seriously: the principle of concentration and the measurement of welfare and inequality'. *Social Choice and Welfare* **32**: 555–74

Elster, J., 1992. *Local Justice*. Cambridge: Cambridge University Press

Evans, R., 1984. *Strained Mercy*. Toronto: Butterworths

Faravelli, M., 2007. 'How context matters: a survey based experiment on distributive justice'. *Journal of Public Economics* **91**: 1399–1422

Fehr, E. and S. Gächter, 2000. 'Cooperation and punishment in public goods experiments'. *American Economic Review* **90**: 980–94

Fleurbaey, M., 1995. 'Three solutions for the compensation problem'. *Journal of Economic Theory* **65**: 505–21

2003. 'On the informational basis of social choice'. *Social Choice and Welfare* **21**: 347–84

2008. *Fairness, Responsibility and Welfare.* Oxford: Oxford University Press

Fleurbaey, M. and F. Maniquet, 2008. 'Fair social orderings'. *Economic Theory* **34**: 25–45

Fleurbaey, M. and P. Mongin, 2005. 'The news of the death of welfare economics is greatly exaggerated'. *Social Choice and Welfare* **25**: 381–418

Fleurbaey, M. and E. Schokkaert, 2009. 'Unfair inequalities in health and health care'. *Journal of Health Economics* **28**: 73–90

Fong, C., 2001. 'Social preferences, self-interest, and the demand for redistribution'. *Journal of Public Economics* **82**: 225–46

Frohlich, N., J. Oppenheimer and C. Eavey, 1987. 'Choices of principles of distributive justice in experimental groups'. *American Journal of Political Science* **31**: 606–36

Gächter, S. and A. Riedl, 2005. 'Moral property rights in bargaining with infeasible claims'. *Management Science* **51**: 249–63

2006. 'Dividing justly in bargaining problems with claims: normative judgments and actual negotiations'. *Social Choice and Welfare* **27**: 571–94

Gaertner, W., 1992. 'Distributive judgments'. *Social Choice and Bargaining Perspectives on Distributive Justice*, eds. W. Gaertner and M. Klemisch-Ahlert: Chapter 2. Heidelberg, Berlin and New York: Springer Verlag

2008. 'Individual rights versus economic growth'. *Journal of Human Development* **9**: 389–400

2009. *A Primer in Social Choice Theory*, rev. edn. LSE Perspectives in Economic Analysis. Oxford: Oxford University Press

Gaertner, W. and J. Jungeilges, 2002. 'Evaluation via extended orderings: empirical findings from Western and Eastern Europe'. *Social Choice and Welfare* **19**: 29–55

Gaertner, W., J. Jungeilges and R. Neck, 2001. 'Cross-cultural equity evaluations: a questionnaire–experimental approach'. *European Economic Review* **45**: 953–63

Gaertner, W. and L. Schwettmann, 2007. 'Equity, responsibility and the cultural dimension'. *Economica* **74**: 627–49

Gaertner, W. and Y. Xu, 2004. 'Procedural choice'. *Economic Theory* **24**: 335–43

2009. 'Individual choices in a non-consequentialist framework: a procedural approach'. *Arguments for a Better World. Essays in Honor of Amartya Sen*, eds. K. Basu and R. Kanbur: 148–66. New York: Oxford University Press

Gamliel, E. and E. Peer, 2006. 'Positive versus negative framing affects justice judgments'. *Social Justice Research* **19**: 307–22

2010. 'Attribute framing affects the perceived fairness of health care allocation principles'. *Judgment and Decision Making* 5: 11–20

Güth, W. and H. Kliemt, 2010. 'What ethics can learn from experimental economics – if anything'. *European Journal of Political Economy* 26: 302–10

Hammond, P., 1976. 'Equity, Arrow's conditions and Rawls's difference principle'. *Econometrica* 44: 793–804

Harsanyi, J., 1953. 'Cardinal utility in welfare economics and the theory of risk-taking'. *Journal of Political Economy* 61: 434–5

1955. 'Cardinal welfare, individualistic ethics and interpersonal comparisons of utility'. *Journal of Political Economy* 63: 309–21

1977. *Rational Behavior and Bargaining Equilibrium in Games and Social Situations*. Cambridge: Cambridge University Press

1978. 'Bayesian decision theory and utilitarian ethics'. *American Economic Review* (Papers and Proceedings) 68: 223–8

Hausman, D., 2000. 'Why not just ask? Preferences, "empirical ethics" and the role of ethical reflection'. Mimeo, forthcoming in a WHO volume

Herne, K. and M. Suojanen, 2004. 'The role of information in choices over income distributions'. *Journal of Conflict Resolution* 48: 173–93

Herrero, C., J. Moreno-Ternero and G. Ponti, 2010. 'On the adjudication of conflicting claims: an experimental study'. *Social Choice and Welfare* 34: 145–79

Herrero, C. and A. Villar, 2001. 'The three musketeers: four classical solutions to bankruptcy problems'. *Mathematical Social Sciences* 42: 307–28

Homans, G., 1958. 'Social behavior as exchange'. *American Journal of Sociology* 63: 597–606

Hurley, J., N. Buckley, K. Cuff, M. Giacomini and D. Cameron, 2011. 'Judgements regarding the fair division of goods: the impact of verbal versus quantitative descriptions of alternative divisions'. *Social Choice and Welfare* 37: 341–72

Johannesson, M. and U.-G. Gerdtham, 1996. 'A note on the estimation of the equity–efficiency trade-off for QALY's'. *Journal of Health Economics* 15: 359–68

Johansson-Stenman, O., F. Carlsson and D. Daruvala, 2002. 'Measuring future grandparents' preferences for equality and relative standing'. *Economic Journal* 112: 363–83

Jungeilges, J. and Th. Theisen, 2011. 'State dependence in sequential equity judgements'. *Social Choice and Welfare* 37: 97–119

Kahneman, D., J. Knetsch and R. Thaler, 1986. 'Fairness as a constraint on profit seeking: entitlements in the market'. *American Economic Review* 76: 728–41

Kalai, E. and M. Smorodinsky, 1975. 'Other solutions to Nash's bargaining problem'. *Econometrica* 43: 513–18

Klemisch-Ahlert, M., 1992. 'Distributive results in bargaining experiments'. *Social Choice and Bargaining Perspectives on Distributive Justice*, eds. W. Gaertner and M. Klemisch-Ahlert: Chapter 5. Heidelberg, Berlin and New York: Springer Verlag.

Kolm, S.-C., 1996. *Modern Theories of Justice*. Cambridge, MA: MIT Press

Konow, J., 1996. 'A positive theory of economic fairness'. *Journal of Economic Behavior and Organization* **31**: 13–35

2001. 'Fair and square: the four sides of distributive justice'. *Journal of Economic Behavior and Organization* **46**: 137–64

2003. 'Which is the fairest one of all? A positive analysis of justice theories'. *Journal of Economic Literature* **41**: 1188–1239

2009a. 'Adam Smith and moral knowledge'. Loyola Marymount University: Department of Economics

2009b. 'Is fairness in the eye of the beholder? An impartial spectator analysis of justice'. *Social Choice and Welfare* **33**: 101–27

Lindholm, L., M. Emmelin and M. Rosén, 1997. 'Health maximization rejected: the view of Swedish politicians'. *European Journal of Public Health* **7**: 405–10

Lindholm, L. and M. Rosén, 1998. 'On the measurement of the nation's equity adjusted health'. *Health Economics* **7**: 621–8

Luce, R. and H. Raiffa, 1957. *Games and Decisions*. New York: Wiley

Magdalou, B. and P. Moyes, 2009. 'Deprivation, welfare and inequality'. *Social Choice and Welfare* **32**: 253–74

Maniquet, F., 1999. 'L'équité en environnement économique'. *Revue Économique* **50**: 787–810

McClelland, G. and J. Rohrbaugh, 1978. 'Who accepts the Pareto axiom? The role of utility and equity in arbitration decisions'. *Behavioral Science* **23**: 446–56

Menzel, P., 1999. 'How should what economists call "social values" be measured?' *Journal of Ethics* **3**: 249–73

Miller, D., 1976. *Social Justice*. Oxford: Clarendon Press

1994. 'Review of Scherer, K. (ed.), Justice: interdisciplinary perspectives'. *Social Justice Research* **7**: 167–88

Mongin, P., 2001. 'The impartial observer theorem of social ethics'. *Economics and Philosophy* **17**: 147–79

Moulin, H., 1987. 'Equal or proportional division of a surplus, and other methods'. *International Journal of Game Theory* **16**: 161–86

2002. 'Axiomatic cost and surplus-sharing'. *Handbook of Social Choice and Welfare, Vol. 1*, eds. K. Arrow, A. Sen and K. Suzumura: 289–357. Amsterdam: North-Holland

Nord, E. 1995. 'The person-trade-off approach to valuing health care programs'. *Medical Decision Making* **15**: 201–8

Nussbaum, M., 2000. *Women and Human Development: The Capabilities Approach*. Cambridge: Cambridge University Press

2006. *Frontiers of Justice: Disability, Nationality, Species Membership*. Cambridge, MA: Harvard University Press

Olsen, J. A. 2000. 'A note on eliciting distributive preferences for health'. *Journal of Health Economics* **19**: 541–50

Pinto-Prades, J.-L. and J.-M. Abellán-Perpiñán, 2005. 'Measuring the health of populations: the veil of ignorance approach'. *Health Economics* **14**: 69–82

Putnam, H., 2008. 'Capabilities and two ethical theories'. *Journal of Human Development* **9**: 377–88

Rawls, J., 1971. *A Theory of Justice*. Cambridge, MA: Harvard University Press

1993. *Political Liberalism*. New York: Columbia University Press

Roberts, K., 1980. 'Possibility theorems with interpersonally comparable welfare levels'. *Review of Economic Studies* **47**: 409–20

Rodriguez-Miguez, E. and J.-L. Pinto-Prades, 2002. 'Measuring the social importance of concentration or dispersion of individual health benefits'. *Health Economics* **11**: 43–53

Roemer, J., 1993. 'A pragmatic theory of responsibility for the egalitarian planner'. *Philosophy and Public Affairs* **22**: 146–66

1998. *Equality of Opportunity*. Cambridge, MA: Harvard University Press

2002. 'Egalitarianism against the veil of ignorance'. *Journal of Philosophy* **99**: 167–84

Rubinstein, A., 1999. 'Experience from a course in game theory: pre- and post-class problems sets as a didactic device'. *Games and Economic Behavior* **28**: 155–70

Samuelson, P. A., 1947. *Foundations of Economic Analysis*. Cambridge, MA: Harvard University Press

Scanlon, T., 1982. 'Contractualism and utilitarianism'. *Utilitarianism and Beyond*, eds. A. Sen and B. Williams: 103–28. Cambridge: Cambridge University Press

Schmeidler, D., 1989. 'Subjective probability and expected utility without additivity'. *Econometrica* **57**: 571–87

Schokkaert, E. and B. Capeau, 1991. 'Interindividual differences in opinions about distributive justice'. *Kyklos* **44**: 325–45

Schokkaert, E. and K. Devooght, 2003. 'Responsibility-sensitive fair compensation in different cultures'. *Social Choice and Welfare* **21**: 207–42

Schokkaert, E. and B. Overlaet, 1989. 'Moral intuitions and economic models of distributive justice'. *Social Choice and Welfare* **6**: 19–31

Schwettmann, L., 2008. 'The acceptance of truncated efficiency'. Martin-Luther-Universität Halle-Wittenberg: Volkswirtschaftliche Diskussionsbeiträge no. 59

Sen, A., 1970. *Collective Choice and Social Welfare*. San Francisco: Holden Day

1973. *On Economic Inequality*. Oxford: Clarendon Press

1979. 'Personal utilities and public judgements: or what's wrong with welfare economics?' *Economic Journal* **89**: 537–58

1980. 'Equality of what?' *Choice, Welfare and Measurement*: 353–69. Oxford: Blackwell

2009. *The Idea of Justice*. London: Allen Lane

Sen, A. and B. Williams, eds., 1982. *Utilitarianism and Beyond*. Cambridge: Cambridge University Press

Smith, A., 1759. *The Theory of Moral Sentiments*. London and Edinburgh

Suzumura, K. and Y. Xu, 2001. 'Characterizations of consequentialism and non-consequentialism'. *Journal of Economic Theory* **101**: 423–36

Swift, A., 1999. 'Public opinion and political philosophy: the relation between social-scientific and philosophical analyses of distributive justice'. *Ethical Theory and Moral Practice* **2**: 337–63

Thomson, W., 2001. 'On the axiomatic method and its recent applications to game theory and resource allocation'. *Social Choice and Welfare* **18**: 327–86

2003. 'Axiomatic and game-theoretic analysis of bankruptcy and taxation problems: a survey'. *Mathematical Social Sciences* **45**: 249–97

Törnblom, K., 1992. 'The social psychology of distributive justice.' *Justice: Interdisciplinary Perspectives*, ed. K. Scherer: 177–236. Cambridge: Cambridge University Press

Traub, S., C. Seidl and U. Schmidt, 2009. 'An experimental study on individual choice, social welfare, and social preferences'. *European Economic Review* **53**: 385–400

Traub, S., C. Seidl, U. Schmidt and M. Levati, 2005. 'Friedman, Harsanyi, Rawls, Boulding – or somebody else? An experimental investigation of distributive justice'. *Social Choice and Welfare* **24**: 283–309

Tsuchiya, A. and P. Dolan, 2007. 'Do NHS clinicians and members of the public share the same views about reducing inequalities in health?' *Social Science and Medicine* **64**: 2499–2503

2009. 'Equality of what in health? Distinguishing between outcome egalitarianism and gain egalitarianism'. *Health Economics* **18**: 147–59

Tsuchiya, A., P. Dolan and R. Shaw, 2003. 'Measuring people's preferences regarding ageism in health: some methodological issues and some fresh evidence'. *Social Science and Medicine* **57**: 687–96

Tversky, A. and D. Kahneman, 1981. 'The framing of decisions and the psychology of choice'. *Science* **211**: 453–8

Ubel, P., 1999. 'How stable are people's preferences for giving priority to severely ill patients?' *Social Science and Medicine* **49**: 895–903

Ubel, P., J. Baron and D. Asch, 1999. 'Social responsibility, personal responsibility, and prognosis in public judgments about transplant allocation'. *Bioethics* **13**: 57–68

Vickrey, W., 1945. 'Measuring marginal utility by reactions to risk'. *Econometrica* **13**: 319–33

Wailoo, A. and P. Anand, 2005. 'The nature of procedural preferences for rational health care decisions'. *Social Science and Medicine* **60**: 223–36

Walster, E., W. Walster and E. Berscheid, 1973. 'New directions in equity research'. *Journal of Personality and Social Psychology* **25**: 151–76

Weymark, J., 1991. 'A reconsideration of the Harsanyi–Sen debate on utilitarianism'. *Interpersonal Comparisons of Well-Being*, eds. J. Elster and J. Roemer: 255–320. Cambridge: Cambridge University Press

Williams, A., 1997. 'Intergenerational equity: an exploration of the " fair innings" argument'. *Health Economics* **6**: 117–32

Yaari, M. and M. Bar-Hillel, 1984. 'On dividing justly'. *Social Choice and Welfare* **1**: 1–24

Young, P., 1994. *Equity in Theory and Practice.* Princeton: Princeton University Press

Author index

Subject index

Printed in the United States
By Bookmasters